P9-EMB-683

BEYOND WINNING

BEYOND WINNING

National Scholarship Competitions
and the Student Experience

THE NATIONAL ASSOCIATION OF
FELLOWSHIPS ADVISORS

• 2003 CONFERENCE PROCEEDINGS •

Edited by Suzanne McCray

Andrew Carnegie Library
Livingstone College
701 W. Monroe St.
Salisbury, NC 28144

THE UNIVERSITY OF ARKANSAS PRESS
FAYETTEVILLE
2005

Copyright © 2005 by The University of Arkansas Press

All rights reserved
Manufactured in the United States of America

09   08   07   06   05   5   4   3   2

Designed by Ellen Beeler

☉ The paper used in this publication meets the minimum requirements of the American National Standard for Permanence of Paper for Printed Library Materials Z39.48-1984.

Library of Congress Cataloging-in-Publication Data

National Association of Fellowships Advisors. Conference (2nd : 2003 : Denver, Colo.)
   Beyond winning : national scholarship competitions and the student experience : the National Association of Fellowships Advisors 2003 Conference proceedings / edited by Suzanne McCray.
      p. cm.
   Includes bibliographical references and index.
   ISBN 1-55728-788-0 (alk. paper)
   1. Scholarships—United States—Evaluation—Congresses. 2. College students—Scholarships, fellowships, etc.—United States—Congresses. I. McCray, Suzanne, 1956– II. Title.
   LB2338.N22 2005
   378.34'0973—dc22

                                                             2004028322

This publication was made possible by the University of Arkansas Honors College.

Contents

Acknowledgments

The conference in Denver would not have taken place without the hard work of the planning committee: Todd Breyfogle, University of Denver; Ann Brown, Ohio University; Lori Goodman, University of Colorado at Boulder; Bob Graalman, Oklahoma State University; Ken Lavin, United States Air Force Academy; Beth Powers, University of Illinois at Chicago; John Richardson, University of Louisville; Richelle Stafne, University of Arkansas; and Mary Tolar, NAFA foundation liaison. Also essential was the cooperative support of foundation members: Louis Blair, executive secretary, Truman Foundation; Mary Denyer, assistant secretary, Marshall Aid Commemoration Commission; Alice Ilchman, director, Jeannette K. Watson Fellowship Program; Warren Ilchman, director, Paul and Daisy Soros Foundation; Walter Jackson, program manager, Fulbright United States Student Programs; Gordon Johnson, provost, Gates Cambridge Trust; Jeffrey Johnson, director, National Science Foundation Graduate Research Fellowship Program; Kristin Kelling, program manager, and Melissa Millage, program assistant, Morris K. Udall Foundation; Helen Mann, vice consul, British Consulate General; Tom Parkinson, program director, Beinecke Scholarship Program; Dell Pendergrast, director, George Mitchell Scholarship Program; Jenny Scott, director of education, British Council USA; Joshua Wyner, chief program officer, Jack Kent Cooke Foundation; and Paul Yost, director, James Madison Memorial Fellowship Foundation.

Special thanks to John Rowett, then warden of Rhodes House, Elliot Gerson, American secretary of the Rhodes Trust, Jonathan Taylor, chairman of the Marshall Aid Commemoration Commission and Robert Cochran, University of Arkansas, for delivering addresses. A special thank you as well to the support provided by the University of Arkansas, making this publication possible, including Chancellor John White and Provost Bob Smith and to the University of Arkansas Press, including director Larry Malley and Anna Moore.

Introduction

Each year thousands of students apply for competitive national and international scholarships. Scholarships like the Rhodes, Marshall, Gates Cambridge, and the Fulbright fund graduate study abroad and are extremely competitive. Each year more than one thousand students apply for the Rhodes or Marshall scholarships. The two scholarships combined support fewer than seventy-five recipients. Students also apply in droves for funding to attend graduate schools in the United States. In 2003, 1,400 students applied for graduate funding from the National Science Foundation Graduate Research Fellowships. Others sought graduate support from (among others) the Department of Energy, the Department of Defense, and the National Institutes of Health as well as the Jack Kent Cooke, Jacob Javits, and Soros foundations. Undergraduate applications also pour into programs like Barry Goldwater, Truman, and Morris Udall. The competition is intense. Students generally have a good understanding of this going into the process, and they are looking for support from informed advisors. A growing number of universities have created an office or designated part of an office to assist these students. The proliferation of support has provided greater access to applicants who may not have applied previously or who have not applied successfully. It has also increased the competition.

With so many students applying for a limited number of awards, advisors ask themselves questions about the goals of their office and the results of their support. Even universities with outstanding win records have many more talented students apply than can possibly receive awards. The National Association of Fellowships Advisors (NAFA) was created not only to increase access to as many deserving students as possible, but also to promote a process that keeps the students' best interests at the center, that encourages self-development, and that makes the learning curve worthy of everyone's effort.

This collection of essays is the result of a NAFA conference held in July of 2003. "Beyond Winning: National Competitions and the Student Experience" was the organization's second biennial conference. The workshop included several celebratory events, marking the one hundredth anniversary of the Rhodes Scholarship and the fiftieth anniversary of the Marshall Scholarship. Both foundations hosted receptions to commemorate their years of service to student leaders, to their communities, and to their countries. The two foundations have served as models for other scholarship programs wishing to encourage academic achievement and public service, and the essays included in this volume from the leaders of those programs make clear the missions and evolving goals of their scholarships, providing critical insights for advisors who may see the foundations as distant and incomprehensible entities. The conference also included representatives from over twenty major foundations who made plenary presentations and met individually with advisors during roundtable sessions. While celebrating the contributions of specific foundations, NAFA members also came to learn about changes in those and other programs and to exchange information and provide support, conducting workshops on a variety of topics from "Managing the Fall Crunch: What Works, What Doesn't" to "Undergraduate Research and Service: Getting Students Involved" to "Gaining and Maintaining Institutional Support for Fellowship Advising: Traditional Approaches and Creative Alliances."

Even though NAFA members assist students competing for a relatively small number of scholarships, they take seriously the charge to grant all students access and have historically been generous in providing information, sharing strategies that work on their campuses, and supporting each other through the exhilarating high points and inevitable low moments that scholarship advising brings. Competition gives way to student interest. Advisors are charged with making sure that talented students have the right information at the right time and are encouraged to take risks that may result in special scholarship opportunities and should result, regardless of the outcome, in a learning experience that is worth the effort. The focus of the conference, this publication, and of NAFA in general is that effort: what is gained beyond winning, for students, for advisors, for foundations, and for institutions.

NAFA is a relatively new organization. It had its beginnings on a hot July weekend in 1999 when 160 scholarship advisors from across the country gathered in Fayetteville, Arkansas, for a conference, "The Truman and Marshall Scholarships: Breaking the Code," designed to make clear Truman and Marshall scholarship program expectations. This event encouraged discussion between the foundations and advisors, prompting exchanges that were valuable to both groups. The Truman Foundation had organized two such conferences in prior years, and has long been a leader in providing clear guidelines for student success.

The conference in Fayetteville was the first time another major scholarship program had been added to the mix. Representatives from other scholarship foundations were also available for consultation, and the benefits were immediately clear. Advisors had access to foundation members who could provide necessary, accurate, and not always apparent information concerning the application process. Advisors could also share concerns and strategies with their peers. A much needed and now much used listserv came out of that conference, but the most important consequence was the idea for a permanent organization for advisors of nationally competitive scholarships generated by Mary Tolar, then deputy executive secretary of the Truman Foundation, and Bob Graalman, director of scholar development and recognition at Oklahoma State University.

The following spring a group of fifteen met in Chicago. That group became the founding board of the National Association of Fellowships Advisors. The organization grew quickly, attracting hundreds of schools, some with already developed fellowships programs on their campuses, others hoping NAFA could help get their campuses moving in the right direction. In 2001, Bob Graalman (NAFA's first president) hosted the first official NAFA conference in Tulsa, Oklahoma. From its inception, NAFA has focused on the students and the benefits of the fellowship application process when the odds of winning may seem remote. A NAFA conference with the focus "Beyond Winning" is thus firmly grounded in NAFA's history and its purpose.

Foundations and advisors are intent on making the scholarship application experience a valuable one that is more about learning and service than it is about winning. The dedication is at times remarkable. John Rowett traveled from South Africa, giving up rare family time, to provide the conference with a stirring reminder that the Rhodes Trust is committed to being an active and responsible member of the global community, just as it asks its scholars to be. His talk was a powerful reminder that outstanding, talented students should always look to giving back, to understanding their own histories and their subsequent obligations. He made clear that foundations must do the same.

Robert Cochran's piece shares stories of victories that arrive in unexpected ways. Jonathan Taylor and Elliot Gerson, keynote speakers for the final conference dinner in Denver, celebrate the anniversaries of their scholarship programs, looking to the future from the perspective of distinguished histories. These talks were highlights of the conference and are included in the first section of this collection. Contributions from British authors have been edited for spelling and punctuation. Each of the essays reflects the style and the opinions of the author, not necessarily that of any foundation.

These addresses are followed by a collection of five essays that were either written for inclusion in the Denver NAFA notebook or were written as the result of conversations at the conference. Ethics is a central theme to all the essays included, and Louis Blair's essay also provides helpful, concrete suggestions for guiding students through the Truman application. These essays are followed by three very informative, instructive reports. Elizabeth Vardaman's report is extremely valuable to those who are trying to understand how the United Kingdom's higher educational system differs from that in the United States. Those wanting to determine the strongest academic programs in the United Kingdom will find this outline's step-by-step process ideal for doing that. The Bellagio report provides advisors insight into the concerns and long-term goals of foundations and the way the scholarship application is evolving. The final report, which provides the results of a survey of the scholarship advising profession, gives us a sense of how our offices look on other campuses. This report provides important information for any university designing a scholarship office.

Scholarship advisors and foundations encourage students to find a passion and expand their dreams, not simply to concentrate on the rewards that winning a major scholarship can bring. All of us have talked with parents of young students who are focused on their child winning a major scholarship. This push often comes before the student has even picked a major. A story by Isaac Beshevis Singer, which I often read to my children, seems to capture this problem perfectly. It is a story of three young friends who love to play together and on one very special evening the heavens open and grant each of them a wish. But they squander their wishes, opting for wisdom, for power, and for adoration. They could have everything, but end with nothing. They begin to cry. An old man discovers the children, who claim the heavens have tricked them.

"Heaven does not play tricks," the old man answers. "You are the ones who tried to play tricks on heaven. No one can become wise without experience; no one can become a scholar without studying. . . . Go home and try to deserve by effort what you wanted to get too easily."

The children go home and follow the old man's advice. All three prosper and live to be elderly citizens in the community. One, who became a great rabbi, finally reveals to the people of his town what had happened to him and his friends so long before. He ends his story by telling them: "For those who are willing to make an effort, great miracles and wonderful treasures are in store."

Great miracles do not come simply by winning a scholarship. Students must have a vision, must enjoy the process of getting where they want to go. Students who look only to the prize trick themselves out of the joy of following a passion where it leads. For those of us who have supported passionate, driven young people, who will do and who will achieve regardless of what immediate rewards come, we know that indeed these students will bring great treasures to us all.

Suzanne McCray, president (2003–5)
National Association of Fellowships Advisors

NAFA Institutional Membership

EXECUTIVE BOARD OF DIRECTORS:
Suzanne McCray, President, University of Arkansas
Beth Powers, Vice President, University of Illinois at Chicago
John Richardson, Treasurer, University of Louisville
Paula Warrick, Secretary, American University
Gordon Johnson, Foundation Liaison, Wolfson College, Cambridge
Bill Beesting, Newsletter coeditor, Florida International University
Jane Curlin, Newsletter coeditor, Willamette University

BOARD MEMBERS:
Mark Bauer, Yale University
James Duban, University of North Texas
Mary Engel, University of Scranton
Cheryl Foster, University of Rhode Island
Mona Pitre-Collins, University of Washington
Elizabeth Vardaman, Baylor University
Stephen Wainscott, Clemson University
Susan Whitbourne, University of Massachusetts–Amherst
Vivienne Wildes, Pennsylvania State University
Debra Young, University of Mississippi

The following institutions are members of the National Association of Fellowships Advisors:

Allegheny College
Alma College
American University
Amherst College
Appalachian State University
Arizona State University

Ball State University
Barnard College
Baylor University
Binghamton University
Bowdoin College
Brandeis University

Brigham Young University
Brown University
Bryn Mawr College
Butler University
California State University, Fullerton
Canisius College
Carnegie Mellon University
Chapman University
Charleston College
City University of New York
City University of New York Brooklyn
    College
Clark University
Clemson University
Colgate University
The College of New Jersey
College of the Holy Cross
The College of St. Scholastica
The College of William and Mary
Colorado State University
Columbia University
Cornell University
Culver-Stockton College
Dartmouth College
Denison University
DePauw University
Eastern Illinois University
Elmira College
Elon University
Emory University
Emporia State University
Fairmont State College
Florida International University
Florida State University
Fordham University
Furman University
The George Washington University
Georgia Institute of Technology
Gettysburg College
Grinnell College

Hamilton College
Harding College
Hendrix College
Holy Family University
Hunter College
Illinois State University
Indiana University of Pennsylvania
John Carroll University
Juniata College
Kalamazoo College
Kansas State University
Kent State University
Kentucky State University
Lafayette College
Lamar University
Lebanon Valley College
Lehigh University
Loyola College in Maryland
Loyola Marymount University
Marist College
Messiah College
Miami University of Ohio
Michigan State University
Middlebury College
Montgomery College
Mount Holyoke College
Muhlenberg College
Murray State University
New Mexico State University
New York University
North Carolina Central University
North Carolina State University
Northwestern University
Oberlin College
Occidental College
The Ohio State University
Ohio University
Oklahoma City University
Oklahoma State University
Penn State Abington

Pennsylvania State University
Pepperdine University
Point Loma Nazarene University
Pomona College
Queens College
Radford University
Reed College
Rice University
Roanoke College
Rochester Institute of Technology
Rollins College
Roosevelt University
Rutgers University
San Francisco State University
Seattle University
Simmons College
Smith College
Southern Illinois University
   Carbondale
St. Edward's University
St. John's College (Annapolis)
St. John's College (Santa Fe)
St. Joseph's University
Stanford University
State University of New York at
   Buffalo
Stony Brook University
Swarthmore College
Syracuse University
Texas A&M University
Texas Tech University
Trinity College
Truman State University
Union College
United States Military Academy
The University of Alabama at
   Birmingham
The University of Arizona
University of Arkansas
University of California, Berkeley

University of California, Davis
University of California, Irvine
University of California, Los Angeles
University of California, Santa
   Barbara
University of Central Florida
The University of Chicago
University of Cincinnati
University of Colorado at Boulder
University of Connecticut
University of Delaware
University of Denver
University of Florida
The University of Georgia
University of Illinois at Chicago
University of Illinois at Urbana-
   Champaign
The University of Kansas
University of Kentucky
University of Louisville
University of Maryland, Baltimore
   County
University of Maryland, College Park
University of Massachusetts Amherst
The University of Memphis
University of Miami
University of Michigan
University of Minnesota, Morris
University of Minnesota, Twin Cities
The University of Mississippi
University of Missouri
University of Missouri—Kansas City
University of Missouri—St. Louis
University of Nebraska—Kearney
University of Nebraska—Lincoln
University of New Hampshire
The University of North Carolina at
   Chapel Hill
The University of North Carolina at
   Pembroke

University of North Dakota
The University of North Florida
University of North Texas
University of Notre Dame
The University of Oklahoma
University of Oregon
University of Pennsylvania
University of Pittsburgh
The University of Portland
University of Puget Sound
University of Rhode Island
University of Rochester
The University of Scranton
University of South Carolina
The University of South Dakota
University of South Florida
University of St. Thomas
The University of Tennessee
The University of Texas at Arlington
The University of Texas at Austin
The University of Tulsa
The University of Utah
The University of Vermont
University of Washington
University of Wisconsin–Whitewater

University of Wyoming
University of Nevada, Las Vegas
Ursinus College
United States Air Force Academy
Valparaiso University
Vanderbilt University
Vassar College
Villanova University
Virginia Military Institute
Virginia Tech University
Wake Forest University
Wayne State University
Wellesley College
Wesleyan University
Western Carolina University
Westminster College
West Virginia University
Wheaton College
Willamette University
William Jewell College
Williams College
Worcester Polytechnic Institute
Wright State University
Yale University
Yeshiva University

1

Reconnection, Responsibility, and Renewal

The Rhodes Trust and the Mandela Rhodes Foundation

JOHN ROWETT

John Rowett, a historian by training, is the chief executive of the Rhodes Trust, the secretary general-designate of the Association of Commonwealth Universities and a professorial fellow of Brasenose College, Oxford. Before becoming the chief executive of the Rhodes Trust, he taught modern American history at Oxford and was responsible for overseeing the development of the Rothermere American Institute, opened in 2001 by former president Clinton. Over the past three years he has, in partnership with Prof. Jakes Gerwel, conceived and developed The Mandela Rhodes Foundation which Nelson Mandela has designated as one of the three legacy organizations that will carry forward his work. This essay is based on a speech Dr. Rowett delivered at the first luncheon of the 2003 NAFA conference at Denver. He wishes to give special thanks to Mary Tolar, who introduced him, and who has made so signal a contribution to the Truman Foundation and to NAFA itself, and whose advice he values.

This year marks both the centenary of the Rhodes Trust and the Rhodes Scholarships and the creation of a new foundation, the Mandela Rhodes Foundation, formed through a partnership between the Rhodes Trust and the Nelson Mandela Foundation, and dedicated to supporting development in Africa.

Cooperation and partnership are the words that also describe the relations between the Gates Trust, the Marshall Commission, and the Rhodes Trust here in the United States. For it to be otherwise would be destructive for the foundations themselves, destructive for the British national interest, but, above all, destructive for the students who apply for our awards. This is the message that the Rhodes Trust has conveyed, and will continue to convey, to all who serve it in the United States in whatever capacity. Each of the major scholarship foundations has its distinctive mandate and its own "brand." However, that does not mean that we stand in any antagonistic or destructively competitive relationship. Concepts of market, or super-bowl competition in this context are quite misplaced.

Each year the Gates Scholarship Trust elects approximately one hundred scholars from the United States; the Marshall Commission elects at least forty scholars from the United States and thirty-two of the ninety-four Rhodes Scholars elected worldwide are chosen in the United States. We know that there are thousands of outstanding American college students who would bring distinction to our respective programs. Our problem is not a shortage of outstanding young Americans, but the limits to the number of scholarships that are available in any one year.

The Rhodes Trust is fortunate indeed in its friends and partners. The centenary of the trust has been marked by celebrations for over one thousand scholars and friends in Cape Town and for two thousand scholars and friends in London and Oxford. At the request of the trustees, I designed the intellectual architecture and oversaw the organization of these

events, which were built around the theme of "An International Conversation on the Building Blocks of a Humane Society."

In this centenary year the Rhodes Trust has entered into a partnership
with former president Mandela to launch the Mandela Rhodes
Foundation. As Mandela stated at the Gala Event in Westminster Hall, the
Foundation was conceived and developed in partnership by the former
Cabinet Secretary of South Africa my friend and colleague, Prof. Jakes
Gerwel, and myself.

In the light of the centenary of the Rhodes Trust, and what the prime
minister called in Westminster Hall the magical linking of the names of
Nelson Mandela and Cecil John Rhodes, it is appropriate to make clear
the purposes of the new foundation and their implications for the Rhodes
Trust.

Like any historian, I believe that context is critical to informed understanding. We need, therefore, to be aware of the historical context in which
the Rhodes Trust developed. It is important to note that the legal name of
the foundation is the Rhodes Trust and not the Rhodes Scholarship Trust.
The scholarship scheme created by Cecil Rhodes has always been at the
heart of the activities of the Rhodes Trust and always will be. However,
from its very beginning the scholarships have not defined the limits of the
activities of the Rhodes Trust.

Cecil Rhodes—that contradictory, deeply flawed, entrepreneurial
genius—was a passionate believer in Africa and its future. Many of his
actions, and some of his beliefs, we find today to be repugnant. Yet whatever view we take of him, there can be no question about his passionate
commitment to South Africa and to Africa more broadly. The history of
South Africa has been profoundly shaped by his actions—for good and
ill.[1] One only has to look around Cape Town to Table Mountain, to
Kirstenbosch Gardens, to Groote Schuur, to the University of Cape Town,
and beyond Cape Town to the wine and fruit farms of Boschendal and
Vergelegen to see the many legacies of Cecil Rhodes. The world's greatest
diamond company is still De Beers, the company that Rhodes founded.

In the years before 1945 the Rhodes trustees were full aware of their
obligation to help to realise at least some of Rhodes's aims and aspirations
for South Africa. They expressed that obligation through varied benefactions in South Africa. After 1945, the Rhodes trustees began to extend
their benefactions in very significant ways to the University of Oxford and

its constituent colleges in addition to their greatest benefaction of all to Oxford: the scholarships.

Something of the history of the Rhodes Trust has been outlined in a volume of essays edited by my predecessor.[2] In his essay in that volume the historian John Darwin analyzes what he called the capture of the trust by "dons with donnish ideas." In the years of high apartheid the benefactions of the trust came to focus almost exclusively upon Oxford. There was increasingly, in the words of Nicky Oppenheimer, a memory loss within the trust and among the scholars, both as to the origins of the money that made possible the scholarships and of Rhodes's own commitment to the development of Africa.

In the late 1980s, the University of Oxford began its first serious fundraising campaign. Over the next fifteen years the Rhodes Trust made benefactions from its endowment of approximately twenty million pounds to the University. The Rhodes Trust was, for example, the largest single contributor to the Rothermere Institute of American Studies. At the same time, in order to benefit the university, the Rhodes trustees expanded significantly the scholarships in the Commonwealth and, for a period, in Europe. One consequence was that the number of scholars in residence came to equal the size of one of the smaller colleges. Increasingly the scholars came to study either doctoral or masters' degrees rather than the second BA, which had historically been the degree of choice, especially for American scholars. The scale of the change was demonstrated in one recent year when not a single one of the thirty-two new American scholars applied to study a second BA. These changes led to ever greater transfers of resources from the trust to the university since the cost of fees for scholars studying for doctorates in the medical school or the business school was three times the level required for those studying for a second BA. Throughout the past decade there has therefore been a very sharp—and continuing—increase in the expenditure of the Rhodes Trust on the scholarships.

During the great bull market of the 1990s, the Rhodes trustees also began a process of re-engagement with South Africa. Major benefactions were made to universities for capital projects, most significantly to the University of Cape Town to build All Africa House, to Rhodes University, and to the Universities of the Western Cape and the Witswatersrand. Smaller benefactions were also made to health and environmental projects and to scholarships in schools and universities.

This was then the context in which three years ago I began, with the full authority of the Rhodes trustees, discussions with Prof. Jakes Gerwel, former president Mandela's chief adviser. The results of what were inevitably lengthy discussions were announced in July 2003 in Westminster Hall by Mandela and hailed in their speeches by the prime minister, the Right Honorable Tony Blair, former president Clinton, Nicky Oppenheimer, the chairman of De Beers, and the Right Honorable Chris Patten, European commissioner for external affairs and the chancellor of both Oxford University and the University of Newcastle.

Why have we entered into this partnership?

We have entered this partnership, which we all see as a full and an equal one, because we believe that it can contribute to the process of historical reconciliation between different and, in the past, opposed traditions. We see it as a powerful symbolic expression of that closing of the circles of history between the colonial past and the democratic present called for by President Mandela in his address to the joint houses of the British Parliament in 1996.

We see our partnership as truly one of equals, entirely consonant with the philosophy of the New Partnership for Africa's Development (NEPAD) and with the view so frequently expressed by former president Clinton that the issue today is not what we can do for Africa but what together we can achieve in partnership with Africa.

We have entered into this partnership because we believe that now is the time for Africa. We believe that Africa will be the twenty-first century's primary test of whether globalization is to be for the benefit of the many rather than the few.

We have entered into this partnership because we believe with Bono that it is an obscenity that the accidents of latitude and longitude should allow my children—and yours—to live full, productive, and satisfying lives yet condemn the child of the laborer toiling on the African farm to a life of bare subsistence deprived of the most basic services and facilities. My son is alive today because of the availability of drugs and treatment denied to his peers in the two-thirds world. The statistics are all too familiar, but they remain horrifying. They should shame all of us living in the one-thirds world: ten million children a year lost to the ravages of diseases that are within our power to prevent if we had the will, the energy and the commitment. Perhaps most shaming of all to a European: in the European

Union we spend $2.20 per day in subsidies on the average cow when 2.8 billion people in our global village live on less than two dollars per day.[3]

We have entered this partnership because we believe that the success of the new South Africa is a necessary condition for the success of the African continent. We believe that the fruits of this partnership can contribute to a better life not only for the people of South Africa, but also for our brothers and sisters across the African continent.

We have entered this partnership because we believe that the South African "miracle" stands as a beacon for the whole global community. It demonstrates that with leadership, with vision, and with commitment it is possible to cross apparently unbridgeable divides.

Every speaker in Westminster Hall dwelt on one salient, if often forgotten, fact. It was the toil of the workers of Africa and the diamonds that they extracted from the soil of South Africa that created the opportunity for every single Rhodes scholar who since 1903 has pursued a dream at Oxford. As Nicky Oppenheimer observed in his speeches to Rhodes scholars at Boschendal and in Westminster Hall, all Rhodes scholars are, by virtue of the scholarship that they have held, inextricably connected to the past, the present, and the future of Africa. In the words of President Clinton, echoed by the Prime Minister, it is entirely appropriate that in the centenary year of the Rhodes Trust some of the wealth taken from the old South Africa should now be returned to support the development of the new South Africa.

The Mandela Rhodes Foundation is the institutional expression of this philosophy of partnership. It has been widely observed that the new foundation has for the first time incorporated both Cecil Rhodes and the Rhodes Trust into the shared history of the new South Africa.[4]

What will be the work of the new foundation and how will it relate to the work of the Rhodes Trust and to the family of Mandela organizations?

Mr. Mandela's legacy work will be carried forward by the Nelson Mandela Children's Fund, the Nelson Mandela Foundation, and the Mandela Rhodes Foundation. Each foundation has its own distinctive mission, though they will work together as a "family" of organizations in carrying forward Mr. Mandela's work. The specific mission of the Mandela Rhodes Foundation will be to develop exceptional leadership capacity in Africa. This mission will be achieved through a Mandela Rhodes Scholarship program for first degree students, a Mandela Rhodes Fellowship program for early to mid-career professionals in all walks of life, a Mandela Rhodes partnership program, an international Mandela Rhodes volunteers program, and a Circles of History forum, at the headquarters of the Foundation at Mandela Rhodes House in Cape Town, dedicated to helping those from conflicted situations around the world to cross apparently "unbridgeable divides."

At the formative stage of the foundation, we expressed the philosophy of the "full and equal partnership" through the appointment of joint chief executives, myself and John Samuel, the chief executive of the Nelson Mandela Foundation. The demands of creating the new foundation have been exceptionally heavy and time consuming and could only be sustained on a short-term basis by those holding other full-time appointments. From the beginning it has been our intention to appoint a full-time chief executive based in South Africa.

We have been able to appoint as our chief executive one of South Africa's leading public intellectuals, Shaun Johnson, who is himself a former Rhodes scholar. Johnson played a prominent and courageous role in the struggle for liberation. Over the past decade he has built a major business career as an editor and, most recently, as the deputy chief executive of the Independent News and Media Group in South Africa. The trustees of the Mandela Rhodes Foundation are deeply grateful for the support of Sir Tony O'Reilly, the chairman of the Independent News and Media Group worldwide, for his support both for Johnson's appointment and for the whole Mandela Rhodes initiative.

The trustees also owe a huge debt of thanks to Nicky Oppenheimer, the chairman of De Beers, who has made the most munificent benefaction of the Rhodes Building in Cape Town, designed by Sir Herbert Baker for Cecil Rhodes, to be the headquarters of The Mandela Rhodes Foundation.

I also wish to acknowledge the great support that we have received from Senator Russ Feingold, Senator Paul Sarbanes, and Senator Dick Lugar in sponsoring the Senate resolution in support of the Mandela Rhodes initiative. It is a matter of great pride to the Rhodes Trust that the three senators who are former Rhodes scholars have demonstrated such support. It is equally a matter of great pride to all of us involved in the initiative that the Senate as a whole has been willing to express its support in this manner. Many in the United States, including Rhodes scholars, provided enormous support for the antiapartheid struggle and for the campaign to free Mr. Mandela. We hope to continue through the Mandela Rhodes Foundation to build ever-closer bonds with the friends of Africa in the United States.

The Rhodes trustees have contributed ten million pounds sterling to launch the foundation. Together with Mr. Mandela and the Nelson Mandela Foundation, we shall seek to raise a further twenty million pounds to form the core endowment. We shall also seek program funding from governments and international bodies, from foundations, and from the corporate sector.

It is clear to all of us who have the privilege to serve the new foundation that we have a unique opportunity to contribute far beyond our financial strength. Our initiative has clearly struck a chord internationally, in part of course because of what Mr. Mandela has come to represent to the whole global community: the personification of hope, of integrity, and of justice and reconciliation in a divided and conflicted world.

Since the gala evening in Westminster Hall we have received hundreds of messages of support and pledges of assistance. Many messages have echoed the judgement of the Prime Minister:

> It is a wonderful thing to contemplate this Mandela Rhodes Foundation. . . . When we see these two names joined together, when we contemplate the extraordinary thing that symbolizes, we can find the energy, the will and the commitment to overcome the differences and difficulties. Nelson Mandela is a person who more than any other single figure establishes the triumph of hope over injustice . . . and when we see the past and the future joined together to give the Rhodes Trust new life for the future, we see the possibility of overcoming the injustices that our world suffers.

All of us involved in the new foundation—and all of the Rhodes trustees—are aware of the expectations aroused by the Foundation. All of us charged with its development are awed by the responsibility that has been given to us, in the words of Mr. Mandela, to "contribute to a better life for the people of South Africa and further abroad on the African Continent."

We are conscious also of the support that we shall require if we are to fulfil these goals and grateful therefore for the support already offered to us by many Rhodes scholars. In his speech in Westminster Hall, former president Clinton spoke on behalf of former Rhodes Scholars when he emphasized the many benefits that they, both individually and collectively, had received from the Rhodes Trust. He said:

> It is altogether fitting, therefore, that we celebrate this one hundredth anniversary of Rhodes' gift to us with another visionary effort that will reach beyond our own mortality. The Mandela Rhodes Foundation will bring some of Rhodes' wealth back to its origins to help to build a new South Africa. . . . Cecil Rhodes' vision gave me the chance to live the life of my dreams. I am profoundly grateful now that the heirs of Rhodes' vision are working with President Mandela to give South Africans, all of them, the same chance to live their dreams.

Those of us involved in running both the Rhodes Trust and the Mandela Rhodes Foundation see no contradiction between giving the future Bill Clintons from around the world the opportunity to live the life of their dreams through the Rhodes Scholarships and giving their counterparts on the African continent the chance to live the life of their dreams.

Indeed, over the past two years we have provided even more facilities in Oxford for Rhodes scholars. We have committed three hundred thousand pounds to a major refurbishment program at Rhodes House to create an IT suite, a common room, and a coffee room for scholars. We have introduced a program of visiting distinguished scholars that brings back to Rhodes House older scholars to act as mentors to current scholars. We have introduced major new lecture programs, in particular in partnership with the Oxford Centre for Islamic Studies, where I have the honor to serve as a trustee, which have brought to Rhodes House, among others, the secretary general of the Commonwealth, the Right Honorable Don McKinnon; the leader of the opposition in India, Sonia Ghandi; Alija Izetbegovic, the president of Bosnia; the chief justice of South Africa, Arthur Chaskalson; and from the United States, Gen. Wesley Clark; former Navy secretary Richard Danzig; Prof. Robert Rotberg; and Tom Friedman, Pulitzer Prize winner and a former Marshall Scholar.

Of course, there are limits to what any foundation can provide and not all current Rhodes Scholars can have everything that they seek. In particular, the trust has to strike a careful balance in Oxford. Rhodes House is not a college and it would be a violation of Rhodes's will to seek collegiate status. All of the changes that we have made are designed to enrich the experiences of scholars while recognizing that, though they have a multiplicity of identities while at Oxford, their departments and colleges should be the primary focus of their activities.

The Rhodes Trust is a wholly independent charitable foundation governed by the will, the 1916, 1929, and 1946 acts of Parliament, and by modern charity law. It is not now, and never has been, a part of the University of Oxford. Its relationship with the university is one of partnership. Oxford faces severe challenges over the coming decade if it is to maintain its position as a leading international university. This has been well illustrated by the considerable body of international comment around the appointment as the next vice-chancellor of Oxford, Dr. John Hood, vice-chancellor of the University of Auckland and the Rhodes Trust's secretary in New Zealand. It may well be that some of the university's responses to its problems will create difficulties for the Rhodes Trust, for example, through ever-increasing fees for overseas students. However, I am convinced that any such difficulties will be dealt with in the spirit of partnership that has developed over the past one hundred years.

The Rhodes Trust has contributed significantly to the world over the past century as it has sought in a variety of ways to realise that part of Rhodes's vision concerning the promotion of international understanding and peace through education. It will continue to do so. But it will do so in a new context in the twenty-first century.

We must recognize that we all live in a new kind of global village. Whether we live in the United States, the United Kingdom, Australia, South Africa, India, or Malaysia, we inhabit a common global village. In that global village we must cultivate a spirit of tolerance and understanding and respect for and appreciation of human diversity. We must remind ourselves of Dr. Martin Luther King's warning: either we learn to live together as brothers and sisters or we shall perish together as fools.

As President Clinton reminded us in his compelling and courageous Nelson Mandela lecture in Johannesburg, where we had gathered to celebrate Mr. Mandela's eighty-fifth birthday:

> We cannot kill or jail or occupy everyone who disagrees with us. We cannot do it. We must build a new kind of global village. We must go beyond the narrow confines of our own interests to the larger confines of our common humanity.

We must act on the wisdom Mr. Mandela expressed in the message on the tapestry of him that now hangs in Rhodes House: "To make peace with an enemy, one must work with an enemy and that enemy becomes your partner."

It is old wisdom for as the Holy Qur'an tells us: "requite evil with good and he who is your enemy becomes your friend."

The values of tolerance, recognition of and celebration of diversity and support for human solidarity are at the heart of the work of the Rhodes Trust. We have sought to give new life and new meaning to these values through our partnership with former president Mandela. We have sought through that partnership to return some of the wealth that established the Rhodes Trust to the new South Africa as it seeks to give a decent and a prosperous life to all South Africans. Above all, in the words of Mr. Mandela, we have sought to contribute to "the advent of a glorious summer of a partnership for freedom, peace, prosperity and friendship."

2

The Rhodes Scholarships

Looking Forward From One Hundred Years

ELLIOT F. GERSON

Elliot F. Gerson is American secretary of the Rhodes Trust. He was a Rhodes Scholar from Connecticut in 1974. A graduate of Harvard and of Yale Law School, he is a former deputy attorney general of Connecticut and was the president of Travelers Insurance Company.

He is now executive vice president of the Aspen Institute and is active in many political and charitable organizations. The following NAFA conference remarks were delivered at a celebration of the fiftieth anniversary of the Marshall Scholarships and the centenary of the Rhodes Scholarships. Jonathan Taylor, chairman of the Marshall Aid Commemoration Commission, and Elliot Gerson were keynote speakers at this event and were introduced by Louis Blair, the executive director of the Truman Foundation.

I am particularly pleased to congratulate the Marshall Aid Commemoration Commission on the fiftieth anniversary of the Marshall Scholarships. The purposes of our scholarships and aspirations are parallel and complementary. My first meeting, upon my appointment as American secretary to the Rhodes Trust five years ago, was with Jonathan Taylor's predecessor about how our fellowship schemes could grow even closer, and that remains the spirit of our meetings together today.

The Rhodes and Marshall scholarships are among the most respected international educational programs in the world, and nothing pleases us more than the creation of new and similar foundations, such as that sponsoring the Gates Cambridge Scholarships. The British scholarships have provided extraordinary benefits to recipients, to be sure, but they also have contributed uniquely—and disproportionately, given the small number of annual recipients—to the most important and beneficial special relationship between nations in modern history. Both Cecil John Rhodes and Gen. George C. Marshall would be proud of their legacies to education and international understanding.

While we Rhodes Scholars know well enough not to entertain the question whether Rhodes or Marshall is the better man to emulate today, we have, on our part, no hesitation in respecting Rhodes for at least bequeathing well, and with a vision that far outlived his mortality. It is the spirit and wisdom of that bequest, made just over a century ago, that we celebrate tonight: that there is great value for our two nations, and the world, for outstanding young citizens of this country to spend two or three of their most formative years studying in Britain.

Dr. John Rowett has emphasized the creation of the Mandela Rhodes Foundation—the remarkable closing of the circle symbolized by the linked names of the most powerful African of the nineteenth century with the greatest African of the twentieth century, or perhaps any century. My aim will be to address what was, and what always will be, the heart of the Rhodes Trust and its primary focus: its scholarships to Oxford University. I will focus on our history and its continuing vitality, a history that will, I am certain, animate the scholarships—and the world—in a remarkably similar way in their second century.

Exactly one hundred years ago, the first American Rhodes scholars were contemplating their imminent trips to New York, including Colorado's own Stanley Kuhl Hornbeck. For most, it was their first time to New York, and for many their first time out of state—and following that, their sea journey to England and to an experience at Oxford they could barely imagine. Their successors a century later (whose biographies you have in our annual newsletter, *The American Rhodes Scholar*) albeit most better traveled, are scarcely less excited about the experience they will soon have amid Oxford's unique splendors.

Cecil John Rhodes was a complex and enigmatic man of an era and place hard for us to understand. He is certainly not someone we can unreservedly admire. As his leading biographer, Rhodes Scholar Robert Rotberg, has written: "he died both genius and rogue, and he served both God and mammon. He was as human, fallible, gentle, charismatic and constructive as he was shameless, vain, driven, ruthless and destructive." As Rotberg put it, "he deserves to be seen in both the bright *and* somber hues of the rainbow." Rhodes was undeniably one of the largest figures of his century, achieving the highest levels of power and influence in business as well as in politics, as few—if any—men have before or since.

Perhaps some of you are familiar with the evolving vision for his legacy as reflected by this physically unhealthy man's many wills and postscripts. Rhodes's vision was born initially in a rather juvenile narcissism, evolving—thank goodness—well beyond his fourth will, when he left most of his fortune to Lord Rothschild and urged that a secret society be established (modeled on the Jesuits but with the words "English Empire" substituted for the words "Roman Catholic Church"). The will that we all benefit from was his eighth, which drew largely on his seventh. It was while developing that seventh will, on a voyage back to the Cape Colony from Britain, that he established the key qualification: "great consideration," he wrote from a stop in Madeira, "should be given to those who have shewn during the school days that they have instincts to lead and . . . which . . . will be likely in after life to guide them to esteem the performance of public duties as their highest aim." Gone were all notions of secrecy, and of empire.

Rhodes perfected this vision in his eighth will, signed just before another sea voyage back to the Cape. He brought together his special admiration for Oxford's residential system and his reverence for its atmosphere and its passion for learning with his vision of the kinds of characteristics that would be necessary if his scholars would change and improve the world. (It is not to be imagined that Rhodes himself showed signs of reverence while in and out of residence at Oriel College, Oxford, some two decades earlier, but that is another story for another day.) Perhaps the clearest statement of his object in the scholarships came in the 1901 codicil, which established the German Rhodes scholarships (created because he believed that the Kaiser was to require the teaching of English in German schools) and where he expressed hope that educational relations among the world's three great powers would help promote international peace.

From the inception of the scholarships, Rhodes scholars received extraordinary attention from the public and from leading journals and newspapers in Britain and in the countries from which Rhodes scholars were drawn. It is easy to forget that the Rhodes Scholars were quite famous, and internationally so, well before Bill Clinton. Let me share one of my favorite examples, a *Punch* cartoon from a number of years ago:

"RHODES SCHOLAR, NO DOUBT!"
Reproduced by permission of the Proprietors of *Punch*

You know you have penetrated popular culture—for good or for ill—when you become the brunt of a cartoon.

Not all thought Rhodes's idea a good one, though. At a Philadelphia lunch with Sir George Parkin (the Rhodes Trust's ambassador to its dominions), none other than Henry James entered what was described as a vehement protest against "the desecration of Oxford by an irruption of young barbarians from Kalamazoo and Wallamarroo, and from Auckland, Arizona and Africa."

But others immediately recognized the great value of the Rhodes bequest. Parkin was met far more hospitably and generously by America's leading politicians and educators, who were not bashful about their views. Teddy Roosevelt, for example, gave him "emphatic" advice about selection committees. He said not to put governors on state selection committees; he "wouldn't trust one of them, not one of them" to make an unbiased selection.

A critical feature of Rhodes's vision was his recognition of the emerging importance of the United States to the future of the world. It was no accident that 96 of the 156 scholars assigned in his will were to American citizens. (One occasionally hears that the disproportion of American scholars is an accident—usually ascribed to a presumption of Rhodes's poor knowledge of geography and history and his supposed presumption that we still had just thirteen states.) But whether due in part to the private urgings of Rhodes's friend, Rudyard Kipling, and Kipling's American wife, or entirely to Rhodes's own intuition, the American scholarships were central to his vision from the outset. And, also contrary to myth, Cecil Rhodes said very clearly that he did not want his scholars to become English in their orientation, noting that he did not want their English sojourns to "withdraw them or their sympathies from the U.S."

One of the most remarkable aspects of our history is the endurance of our criteria, which were quite radical at the time. The qualities he sought in his will are all valuable today, in all our worldwide constituencies: academic excellence, healthy vigor, care for the weak, and ability to assume leadership.

Indeed, in addition to the endurance of the criteria, it is remarkable how little change there has been administratively in a century. Some adjustments have been required, to be sure. Few Americans could pass the early qualifying exam in Latin and (especially) Greek. Several agreements between the trustees and the university between 1909 and 1919 eased this difficulty and by 1920 both the Latin and Greek examinations had been dropped. The district system was developed in the 1920s because of the imbalance in numbers and quality across the states, but only over the objections of governors and a proposed Senate resolution. The district system has been modified again slightly in the last five years—again to redress an imbalance in state numbers.

Of course the most significant change was the overdue but necessarily legal change—requiring an act of Parliament—to admit women in 1976. No legal change was necessary—only attitudinal—to admit black Rhodes Scholars on a regular basis. The will explicitly made race no bar (though almost certainly Rhodes did not contemplate black scholars). Pennsylvania elected Alain Leroy Locke in 1907, and after formal protests by southern Rhodes Scholars and the Rhodes trustees' fear that southern students would no longer apply, no American black was elected again until forty years ago, unquestionably a stain on our history.

So what has been accomplished by the Rhodes scholarships in this century, and what will be in the next? Well, it is entirely fair to say that the international fellowships now being offered—as well as the nation's ubiquitous junior years and semesters abroad—are Rhodes's direct legacy, as are many (if not all) of the other scholarships represented at this conference. Senator J. William Fulbright credited his own Rhodes scholarship for the scholarships that bear his name. The Marshall Scholarships, of course, chose similarly selective criteria, and my predecessor was consulted by the British Foreign Office as the scholarships were established. The Mitchell Scholarship organizers asked my office to help design their competition, and it was my privilege to be the founding chair of their selection committee. And yet another example: Bill Gates's late mother, Mary Gates, served for many years as chair of our Washington state and northwest Rhodes District selection committees; that experience influenced her husband, Bill Gates Sr., as the Gates Cambridge Scholarships were formulated by them and Cambridge officials.

But the ultimate success of the Rhodes scholarships is measured, and will continue to be measured, by the lives and careers of its recipients, by the strong links between the United Kingdom and the United States, and by the continuing and undeniable verity of Rhodes's vision: that international educational exchange makes for a better world. And now, the vision of the Mandela Rhodes Foundation will magnify that contribution and assure that even more of it is redirected to the continent where Rhodes's wealth originated, and to where many of his scholars will choose to engage in "the world's fight," to use Rhodes's now famous phrase.

After the illegal Jameson raid into the Transvaal, Rhodes was forced to resign from a position involving the effective governance of Rhodesia. During the parliamentary debates about that ill-fated raid, Rhodes said he feared the country might lose his name. "They can't change the name of a country, can they?" he said. Well, of course, they can and they did. Where once was Rhodesia we now have Zimbabwe and Zambia, and in one of the most beautiful spots of Zimbabwe, indeed of anywhere in Africa, Cecil John Rhodes lies buried. But while his country name is gone, Cecil John Rhodes remains known worldwide for his scholarships.

Sir Anthony Kenny, former warden of Rhodes House, has written of Rhodes that the scholarships were "the best of all things he did in his full and tumultuous life." And we can say now, with the confidence afforded by the passage of one hundred years, just how great and enduring a thing establishing the scholarships was. I have no doubt that the same thing will be said a century from now, with even more dividends having been paid—to world understanding, to peace, to the central value of education, and to greater equity among peoples, as well as to the myriad fields of scholarly accomplishment and committed leadership of several more generations of Rhodes Scholars.

3

Marshall Scholarships

Moving into the Twenty-first Century

JONATHAN TAYLOR

Jonathan Taylor has been chairman of the Marshall Commission since 2000. He is also chairman of the governing body of the School of Oriental and African Studies (University of London), chairman of the Booker Prize Foundation and of the Council of the Caine Prize for African Writing, and chairman of Paintings in Hospitals. He was until his retirement chairman and chief executive of Booker plc, an international food and agribusiness company. He has received bachelor's and master's degrees from Oxford University, where he is an honorary fellow of Corpus Christi College and an honorary curator of the Bodleian Library. Taylor provided one of the two keynote addresses for the 2003 NAFA conference, marking the fiftieth anniversary of the Marshall Scholarships and the centenary of the Rhodes Scholarships.

A major anniversary, whether fifty years or one hundred years, is a time to look back as well as forward. In 1947 I was twelve and at a boarding school in England because my parents were in Africa. The winter of 1946–47 in Europe was one of the worst ever. I remember vividly being both very cold and very hungry. There was little fuel for any heating, and food was still rationed at or below wartime levels. The Royal Airforce had to drop supplies to villages and communities that were cut off; power cuts led to short-time working; fishing fleets could not leave port. All this in the context of an economy that was so depleted and exhausted by the war that in the summer British forces had to be withdrawn from Greece, where they were fighting a communist takeover. Continental Europe, war-ravaged, was in equally bad shape.

Help came very quickly from the United States in the form of the Marshall Plan. But first let me say a few words about Gen. George C. Marshall, who was by then secretary of state. The adjectives used to describe George Marshall have a certain consistency: modest, honest, trustworthy, loyal, capable, professional, disciplined, firm, courteous. His contribution to victory in the Second World War goes without saying. He recruited, mobilized, trained, equipped, and shipped the vast forces for war in Europe and the Pacific as Army chief of staff. He could have been supreme allied commander in Europe, but as Roosevelt said "you know, I do not think I could sleep well at night with you out of the country," and so the European job went to Eisenhower. He also had an important role in restraining Churchill's wilder and over-adventurous military ideas.

After the Second World War came the cold war, and Marshall was called back to serve as secretary of state under Truman. In 1947, the year of my frozen winter, came the Truman Doctrine and the Marshall Plan, the twin pillars of a symbiotic relationship which still continues, I believe, in the warm understanding between the Marshall and Truman Scholarship programs. Marshall's speech to the graduating class at Harvard in 1947 took only ten minutes, but it changed the world. "It is logical" he said, "that the United States should do whatever it is able to do to assist in the return of normal economic health in the world without which there can be no political stability and no assured peace." Later he added, "Our policy is directed not against any country or doctrine but against hunger, poverty, desperation, and chaos." The words still resonate today.

The phrase "Marshall Plan" lives on, and we still talk about Marshall Plans for Africa, the Middle East, Afghanistan, or wherever. It is shorthand for massive economic aid and technical assistance delivered quickly and without too many strings attached.

The United Kingdom was far and away the largest beneficiary of the Marshall Plan, but other countries in Western Europe also benefited, notably Germany. By the time the Marshall Plan was completed in 1951, the United States had spent in aid the equivalent of about 1.2 percent of its Gross National Product. In contrast, the GNP of the participating countries grew by over 32 percent in the same period. The indirect effects were even more far-reaching, leading eventually to the creation of the European Union. Marshall went on to receive the Nobel Peace Prize before he died in 1959.

Britain's gratitude for the Marshall Plan took the form of a scholarship program, instituted fifty years ago. The scholarship program was designed by Roger Makins, later Lord Sheffield and ambassador to the United States, whose name lives on in the Marshall Sheffield post-doctoral fellowship program. The scholarships were based loosely on the Rhodes, with the important differences that scholars could go to any university in Britain and the program was open to women as well as men (Rhodes then being all male). The first cohort comprised twelve scholars. At the time George Marshall wrote "A close accord between our two countries is essential to the good of mankind in this turbulent world of today and that is not possible without an intimate understanding of each other."

Let me now fast forward fifty years, with 1,300 scholars having traveled from the United States to the United Kingdom. The high point of our anniversary celebration was the inaugural award of our first Marshall medal to American secretary of state Colin Powell. The presentation was made by His Royal Highness the Prince of Wales, who is patron of the Marshall Alumni Association. The careers of the two soldier/statesmen, Marshall and Powell, have a nice symmetry.

Our other plans for the anniversary are longer term in nature. First, we want to ensure that all Marshall Scholars who have a good academic case for doctoral study will have available funding for a third year in the United Kingdom. We have achieved this for the past four years, and in 2003 we offered third year funding to twenty out of forty scholars. Second, we want to increase gradually the number of scholarships available from forty to fifty (for the fiftieth anniversary). Despite these difficult economic times, we are making reasonable progress in this direction and in fall of 2003 we offered forty-four scholarships as opposed to forty in 2002.

Third, we want to bring to the attention of scholars centers of academic excellence in the United Kingdom outside Oxford, Cambridge, and the London School of Economics, which seem to be the chosen destinations of some 80 percent of Marshall Scholars.

Hitting all three objectives is our new partnership arrangement with Imperial College London. Each year there will be up to four jointly funded Imperial Marshall Scholarships for doctoral study over a three-year period. A similar arrangement is in place with Nottingham. We also have a new arrangement with the National Institutes of Health, which will provide for up to three jointly funded and jointly supervised scholarships in bioscience and medical science again for doctoral study over a four-year period. We also have plans for partnership arrangements with other high quality United Kingdom institutions such as Queen Mary London, Royal Holloway, and Queens University Belfast. Two additional government-funded Texas Marshall Scholarships for Texas universities are also particularly welcome. We are confident that we can increase the number of scholarships available, some through partnership arrangements, without any diminution or compromise in the quality of the Marshall brand because we will always maintain control over the selection process and the administration and well-being of the scholars.

A further objective has been to diversify the sources of the scholars in the United States, and it was good that last year we selected four scholars from four universities that had never previously provided a Marshall Scholar.

When we visited the NIH in Washington earlier this year, one of the scientists there told us about his time working in a research laboratory in Oxford. With him in the lab was a British scientist who always seemed to turn up much later in the morning, took longer lunch breaks, and left earlier in the evening. Eventually the NIH scientist asked him what he was doing all the time when he was not in the lab, to which the reply was "I spend a lot of time thinking what experiments I do not need to do."

I hope that the Marshall experience involves thinking outside the box, perhaps moving outside the box, discovering new challenges, and finding new mountains to climb. We should not be satisfied with obvious, shallow, superficial, and simplified forms of knowledge, but accentuate the importance of subtlety, nuance, depth, background, and complexity.

So who are the 1,300 Marshall Scholars? They are in academia (occasionally heading up universities), they are in journalism (occasionally winning Pulitzer Prizes), they are in the administration and government (occasionally in the cabinet), they are lawyers and in the judiciary (occasionally a Supreme Court justice), they are in the armed forces (occasionally a general), they are in business and finance. But they are also in the voluntary, not-for-profit sector. I was particularly impressed that the class project for 2003's arrivals was the restoration of the public library in Kigali destroyed in the civil war in Rwanda. Our Marshall Scholarship volunteer program is described on our Web site.

Perhaps a typical Marshall Scholar is the fictional deputy director of communications in the television series *The West Wing*. He arrived with a description that he had been a Marshall Scholar at Cambridge, England. Perhaps the hallmark of a Marshal Scholar is quiet achievement, as it was for George Marshall more than fifty years ago. I hope it will continue to be so.

4

Victory's Incognito Arrival

ROBERT COCHRAN

Robert Cochran, a Guggenheim fellow and three-time Fulbright Scholar, is professor of English and director of the Center for Arkansas and Regional Studies at the University of Arkansas. He has written numerous books on such diverse topics as Samuel Beckett, Ozark folklorist Vance Randolph, Arkansas music, a folk painter, and an African American photographer. He has produced three documentary videos and several CD collections of Arkansas music. He regularly sits on campus selection committees and interview panels. The essay below is based on the remarks Cochran delivered at the first main evening event at the NAFA conference.

Last July I was in St. Petersburg with my sixteen-year-old son. We spent our days together strolling the corridors of the Hermitage, and in the early mornings I jogged by myself along the Neva, passing unconscious drunks and, in one grisly instance, a just-mugged corpse. (These are appropriate associations—St. Petersburg, remember, was the glamorous city of Peter the Great and Pushkin's *Eugene Onegin,* but also home to the surreal nightmares of Gogol and Dostoevsky's brutal slum.)

And in fact St. Petersburg also provides me with a scintillating epigraph —from "The Nose," Nikolai Gogol's famous short story. When the barber Ivan Yakovlevich discovers the nose of his regular customer, Collegiate Assessor Kovalyov, in his breakfast bread roll, his initial recourse is to the comforts of logical analysis and taxonomy: "This is an impossible occurrence," he thinks. "After all, bread is something baked, and a nose is something altogether different."

In the spirit, then, of such incongruous juxtapositions, I'll plunge to my real subject, to a double-barreled comparison between traveling and teaching, two things I do, and mentoring applicants for fellowships and scholarships, the thing advisors do. "Beyond Winning," I was informed in St. Petersburg, is the focal theme of the NAFA conference and of the organization in general, and I was moved by such a notion, as I strolled the Hermitage and jogged the Neva, to consider what at bottom constitutes an experience worthy of victory's sonorous name. Is victory at its heart no more than triumph, requiring for its celebratory dance only the prostrate form of its radically subordinated partner defeat? Or is there in true victory something enduring, some continuing presence, a nontransient effect upon our lives? And if so, how might such victory appear, be recognized as such, by a traveler, a teacher, a fellowships advisor?

To consider these matters, I will revert now to anecdote, the better to appreciate victory's depths. As it happens, I have two; both involve traveling and teaching. In 1985 we went to Romania for a year—I was a Fulbright lecturer. We were three—my wife Suzanne, myself, our two-year-old daughter Masie. Romania was then a grim place, brutally ruled by a 1950s-style Stalinist thug named Nicolae Ceausescu, and we were classic innocents abroad, ignorant in every way.

Early in our stay, we waited in a queue to purchase our lunch—pale, grey-colored, mystery-meat hot dogs. We stood out—by our clothes, by our clumsy hesitations in ordering, by our possession of large-denomination bills, most of all by our lovely blonde child—so people engaged us in conversation. Briefly. I very much welcomed these encounters—they gave me my first opportunities to try out the "survival Romanian" I had acquired in a four-week course in Washington. But we soon noticed a bizarre phenomenon we later called "magical vanishing." In every conversation we were soon asked about our home. "Where is your home?" "What is your nation?"

"We're Americans," we replied, "just off the train." Whereupon our new friends instantly disappeared. There were laws, of course, barring Romanians from even conversing with foreigners, but we were newly arrived, yet to learn that chats with Germans or Swedes, even with Canadians, were sometimes tolerated. But Americans were regarded as uniquely virulent and contagious interlocutors.

Anyway, there we were, in the queue, in search of grey hot dogs, as person after person spoke, greeted, welcomed, questioned, evaporated. These were cowed people, and we were anathema, excommunicate. Then, at Suzanne's side, suddenly, victory arrived incognito. She was a young woman, and in her hand was a small pair of white children's socks. "Pentru copii," she said, pointing at Masie, handing the socks to Suzanne. "For the child." Then she too was gone. We were immediately moved and grateful, of course, but most of our year passed before we learned enough to more fully appreciate her gesture's bravery and generosity. As we did, her moment grew and sharpened in our memories, and eventually it took its rightful place at the whole experience's apex—hers was victory's face, as we encountered it in Romania.

My second anecdote comes from the early summer of 2003. That year I had one of my best recent ideas, though as often happens it originated in levity. I developed an American Studies class for the summer session called "The Culture of the Great Plains," which included in the final week a class trip. We read in and about Willa Cather and Lewis and Clark, Mari Sandoz and John Steuart Curry, Kathleen Norris and Ian Frazier. We watched *Powwow Highway, Badlands,* and Buster Keaton's *Go West.* And then we took off, in University of Arkansas vans, for a week-long odyssey to Red Cloud, Nebraska, the Sand Hills and the Badlands, Wall Drug and the Crazy Horse monument. We spent a night in a Benedictine monastery. (I need to interrupt here to explain this great idea's beginnings in send up and parody. Every semester, teaching in our honors courses, I listen as various faculty members appear to shill for their summer study-abroad courses—classics profs headed for Greece and Rome, European studies honchos off to Paris and Vienna, Asian Studies folks with slides of last year's cohort at the Great Wall, the Shakespeare guy doing London and Stratford. That is when it came to me, the notion of an Anti-Grand Tour, and the poster I designed made the joke explicit: "Just imagine," it read, "while your classmates take in the Parthenon, the Louvre, the terra cotta warriors, YOU [I capped this word] can be in Kansas, Nebraska, and South Dakota instead.")

By plan, this trip's grand finale was a dinner at Arthur Bryant's barbecue restaurant in Kansas City. A fortunate few may know this place—Calvin Trillin once called it the finest restaurant in the world. It also once featured the funkiest jukebox in America—scores of soul and rhythm and blues classics, James Brown at top volume as you stuffed yourself—but this treasure has disappeared, I am sorry to report. But the barbecue was as good as ever, and we had a fabulous time. One graduate student had warned me repeatedly that she'd be a tough sell on the "best barbecue in the world" claim—"I'm from Texas," she said. "I've eaten world-class barbecue." But there she sat, across the table, plate emptied, wide smile on her face. "OK," she said, laughing. "You win. This is unbelievable. Turns everything else I ever ate to Alpo."

But then, into this Kansas City triumph, as suddenly as into the defeat in Bucharest, victory rounds the corner, in disguise as usual. It's no young woman this time, a child's socks in her hand, but a middle-aged guy, a construction worker in muddy rubber boots, worn out by the day and its labors. His dark face is grim—he looks weary, even in Arthur Bryant's. When I spot him I'm walking my co-teacher's one-year-old boy around, so she can eat. There we are, moving toward each other, the construction worker holding his take-out in a bag, me reaching down so the little guy can hold my finger.

When he takes us in his whole face lights up in a smile, and as he goes by, never breaking stride, he reaches down and tousles the little boy's hair. It is every bit as brief as the Romanian moment eighteen years earlier, but this time I know right away it will last as long. Eighteen years from now, if I'm still conscious, this single image, dark fingers nestled in the blond curls, a blessing more powerful than any prelate's, I insist, will still be vivid, will yet serve as the whole venture's metonymic center, just as the woman with the socks, the woman who would not be cowed, who would break the law that forbade her to welcome a guest who had come a long way, still serves to summon and justify our year in Romania.

So there you have it, noses and bread loaves compared, essences of true victory intimated. Don't mistake the accidental for the essential—both anecdotes, I know, involve children. Both also involve food. Those are just my idiosyncrasy; I am a glutton besotted by children. But in each instance entire adventures—the year in Romania and the class trip—were most enduringly validated by apparently peripheral and wholly unanticipated moments.

Victory's heart, all this says, may be far removed from the moment of triumph, arms raised on the stand and the anthem playing. Victory is the god in disguise, the gift that comes in the night, the goal reached without striving. For all of us who work with our institution's best and brightest, real victory, this little meditation suggests, appears suddenly, obliquely, without fanfare, disguised as quotidian. Real victory plays out over years, decades, perhaps even a lifetime, long after the newspaper stories lauding the big winners are lining litter boxes. The woman in Romania gave our daughter socks in 1985—that happened twenty years ago, and if anything the moment is more vivid today than it was at the time. True victory is experience redeemed—a past that stays present and informs a future. It is always a surprise, always understood as beyond deserving, always encountered as a form of grace. It is your good fortune and privilege, in your daily work, to lead other people toward it, and in that leading find it for yourselves.

5

Having a Winner Every Time in the Truman Scholarship Competition

LOUIS H. BLAIR

Louis H. Blair has devoted his entire professional career to public service. As a staff member for the president's science advisor, he held political appointments in the White House during the Ford and Carter administrations. He worked for the United States Senate Committee on Commerce, Science and Transportation. He consulted for the Organization for Economic Cooperation and Development in Paris, the United States Environmental Protection Agency, the Appalachian Regional Commission, and the Commonwealth of Virginia. For seven years he conducted research at the Urban Institute on ways to enhance the productivity of state and local governments. He has been the executive secretary of the Truman Scholarship Foundation since 1989. In the course of serving on selection panels for the Truman, Marshall, Gates Cambridge, Rhodes, and Coca-Cola scholarships, he has interviewed nearly four thousand of America's most promising young people and has systematically studied the characteristics for advancement in the written and oral parts of each of the scholarship competitions.

As the director of a program that grants two million dollars in scholarship assistance each year, I get many warm letters. The most satisfying ones are those that come from persons who were not selected as Truman Scholars, but who recognize themselves as winners nonetheless.

The following is from a Truman contestant, passed on by the faculty representative of an institution that has never had a Truman Scholar and rarely has a Truman finalist, but frequently has participants in the Truman competition.

> As you may know, Tuesday the finalists for the Truman Scholarship were posted. Unfortunately, I did not make it to the interview round. You are right; the finalists look like tough competition!
>
> I just wanted to thank you for giving me the opportunity to try for this scholarship. There is no disappointment in not making it, when you give it your best shot and learn something in the process. This has been a learning experience, in that I see where I am, what things I need to improve, and long-term goals I need to set. I'm constantly on the lookout, now, for new ways to get involved in my career interests, understand what I truly want for myself in the future, and how this can be accomplished.
>
> Thank you so much for all the time you have spent helping me. You've been absolutely wonderful. When professors whom I respect show such support and encouragement for my future it makes me realize I sometimes underestimate my ability, and that is perhaps the only thing holding me back. Your enthusiasm has created quite a positive difference in my attitude and in my life and I want you to know how much that is appreciated!
>
> —A 2003 Truman candidate

While I receive relatively few letters of such careful construction and such gracious appreciation, I receive a dozen or more each year sharing similar sentiments. I hear often from Truman faculty representatives that they have received warm notes of gratitude.

General Benefits of the Truman Application Process

The foundation conducts lots of surveys, as active faculty representatives know. I have a program evaluation background, largely from having spent more than a decade conducting assessments of public programs as a staff member at the Urban Institute and at two organizations whose responsibilities were to assess the performance of government programs. I believe in conducting surveys to get objective opinions from clients on how well they feel government programs have served them.

In the mid 1990s, the foundation gave a grant to Dr. Larkin Dudley of the Center for Public Administration and Policy at Virginia Tech to conduct follow-up interviews with "unsuccessful" Truman candidates. Her charge was to conduct twenty- to thirty-minute structured telephone interviews with Truman candidates one year after they had submitted an application and not been selected for a Truman and to find out what they thought about the experience. Roughly half of the candidates surveyed had not been invited for a Truman interview although they had clearly worked hard on their applications.

The bottom line question was the following:

Question: "Thinking about your experience with the Truman Scholarship, are you satisfied that you applied for a Truman Scholarship even though you were not selected?"
Responses [N=127]:

Very satisfied	67 percent
Somewhat satisfied	24 percent
In effect, "Wish I had never heard of the Truman Scholarship Foundation"	9 percent

These results are consistent with the findings of recent surveys. Every year, the Truman Foundation surveys candidates who reach the interview stage. In the 2003 Truman selection and interview cycle, 221 finalists were surveyed at the end of the day of their interview. All finalists reported one or more substantial benefits from the application process, the most frequently mentioned being that the process:

Clarified my career goals and objectives	82 percent
Gave me a better understanding of my policy topic	75 percent
Helped me begin serious planning for graduate school	64 percent
Made me more aware of my values and interests	63 percent

General satisfaction with the Truman application and interview process:

Very satisfied	73 percent
Somewhat satisfied	26 percent
Generally dissatisfied	1 percent

The Truman Scholarship application has been designed to be a structured diagnostic tool to help students think about what is important to them and to get them to begin planning for their post-baccalaureate careers in terms of graduate education and work before and after graduate education.

Careful, sustained effort is required to put together a credible application. Students who devote extensive amounts of time to an academic exercise with faculty supervision and guidance should grow in maturity.

What are some ways that Truman faculty representatives can make Truman applicants winners every time, even if they ultimately receive that skinny letter in the mail or click on to the Web site and fail to find their name among the list of students to be interviewed for the Truman Scholarship?

Sell the program appropriately during the recruitment of candidates. Let them know such things as:

What winning means

The odds of being selected as a Truman Scholar are long: typically there are six hundred applicants and only seventy-six Scholars selected. Winning does not mean only being selected as a Truman Scholar. Winning includes:

- Learning about themselves through the process
- Gaining better presentation skills
- Making suitably ambitious plans for the future
- Getting prepared for applications in the senior year, for other post-baccalaureate fellowships, or for admission to competitive graduate schools.

A substantial amount of work is required to prepare a good application

Candidates who advance to the interview phase of the Truman competition frequently spend as much time on the Truman process as they spend on a three-hour demanding course.

You and other faculty will be there to help and encourage them along the way

The Truman application requires a great deal of introspection and extreme care in answering the questions and presenting the material. Many students will not be used to doing such work. Candidates often get bogged down or discouraged.

Truman candidates are being honored by representing the university

You believe that they have the values, experiences, intellect, and persona to proudly represent your institution before a panel likely to include a United States Court of Appeals judge (one step removed from the U.S. Supreme Court), one or two university or college presidents, a leader in the public service, and a former Truman Scholar on a fast track to prominence in the public service.

Understand what the Truman Foundation is seeking in terms of candidates and written materials

While useful for all involved, the process is likely more satisfying in the long run if you work with the types of candidates the foundation seeks and if you understand what parts of the application are most critical in the review.

What does the foundation seek? It seeks people who are intent upon becoming change agents to improve the operations of government agencies and to establish or enhance the operations of existing nonprofit and advocacy groups that either serve people (especially those in need of assistance) or protect resources. The foundation has no preferences as to whether Scholars aspire to work at the local level or the national level, in the United States or abroad, in low profile or high profile positions. It does care that the bottom line for the student is service and improvement of conditions for others.

There are two types of students who you should give attention to recruiting:

Outspoken advocates full of passion, piss, and vinegar, whom you would gladly recommend to lead a movement for change, perhaps taking on entrenched interests on behalf of causes in which they believe and having some chance to make a difference.

Persons of the quality you would recommend to serve as a student trustee of the university or student member of a presidential or dean search committee where the person could work well with persons who are his/her seniors and could have some influence.

The Truman selection process is not grades driven. The foundation's selection panels care far more about the quality of the candidates' public service record and ability to bring about change than about grades. The foundation does care that the Truman Scholars will be good students in whatever graduate program they attend. The foundation is not giving priority to people who will become editors of the law review or otherwise first in their graduate school class. If you do not have a good sense of what the foundation seeks, get on the Web site http://www.truman.gov and browse around. If this exploration raises specific questions, contact me at lblair@truman.gov.

Make clear to students expectations for success

These are likely to be their serious commitment to the application, willingness to consider advice and constructive criticisms that you and other faculty/staff offer, submission of a good product that reflects favorably on the student and on the institution, openness to growth during the process, and graciousness in thanking all of the persons who worked on their behalf.

Be accessible to candidates

Successful Truman candidates (i.e., those who put together polished applications and have sufficient credentials to get to a Truman interview) will spend up to one hundred or more hours on their Truman applications and policy proposals. They will need encouragement to keep going and help in refining drafts. Often, a few weeks before the deadline, candidates reach a stage of high anxiety—referees have not provided letters, responding to item fifteen is difficult, they cannot get the policy recommendation onto one page, and similar types of complaints. They need guidance and reassurance.

Be there for them and recognize this can be a serious time demand on you. Recently a Truman faculty representative who is vice president for student affairs at a California university said to me:

> Louis, I have some bad news and some good news. First the bad news, we have no Truman Nominees this year. The good news is that I was able to get my work done for the university in the month leading up to the Truman deadline.

While this might be a bit of an exaggeration, the application process is time demanding for the candidate and for the faculty representative.

Find ways for the institution to recognize the candidates as persons of whom the institution is truly proud, regardless of the outcome

Recognition can come in a number of ways, such as: dinner with the president of the institution for all nominees for major scholarships regardless of the outcome, a specially selected book with a personal inscription from a faculty member, modest funding for the senior thesis or a summer travel grant, and academic credit for having gone through the process.

Put the Truman outcome in perspective

This is not a life or death outcome. While winning can increase the speed with which these future change agents attain their goals and ambitions, failure to come home with the Truman should not affect their ability to get into and find a way to cover the costs of a first-class graduate institution nor diminish their likelihood of achieving their long term goals.

Every year, talented Truman applicants who were not successful go on to achieve success and distinction in other highly competitive scholarship programs. Sometimes they are not exactly what the Truman seeks to reward but they are what the Rhodes, Marshall, Mitchell, or other programs seek. Sometimes the candidate has not put together a stellar application or a compelling interview for the Truman but does so for scholarships a year later. Typically a dozen "unsuccessful" Truman applicants each year will be selected in subsequent years for a Rhodes, Marshall, or Mitchell.

Encourage the students to use the process to build for the future

Little if any of the work that goes into the Truman application is wasted, even for persons not selected. The response to question fifteen: "what additional personal information do you wish to share with the Truman Scholarship Foundation" can be the basis for a personal statement for a post-baccalaureate fellowship. Responses to other requests for information on the application (such as "describe one specific example of your leadership," "describe a recent particularly satisfying public service activity," "describe the problem or need of society you want to address when you enter public service," "describe the graduate program you intend to pursue if you receive a Truman Scholarship," "what do you hope to do and what position do you hope to have upon completing your graduate studies) should provide much of the structure for applications to graduate school. Answers to these questions, along with the response to the policy proposal, should help candidates determine the type of graduate school education most appropriate for them.

Advisors cannot guarantee the selection of their candidates as a Truman Scholar, no matter how strong or how well they meet the criteria above. By understanding the Truman program and following this plan with an engaged, dedicated candidate, advisors can guarantee nominees a winning experience in the Truman Scholarship competition.

6

Scholarships: Reward, Opportunity, Obligation?

GORDON JOHNSON

Gordon Johnson is the president of Wolfson College, Cambridge, and provost of the Gates Cambridge Trust. *He is also university lecturer in the history of South Asia and director of the Centre of South Asian Studies. His main research interests are the history of India since the late eighteenth century, and the history of the University of Cambridge from the mid-nineteenth century. His publications include* University Politics: F.M. Cornford's Cambridge, Advice to the Young Academic Politician, *and* The Cultural Atlas of India. *He is a member of the University Council and chairs a number of university committees, including in particular the syndicate of Cambridge University Press.*

From the very earliest times, students have been awarded scholarships to attend universities. In essence, scholarships have always been a simple contract: they allow a talented person to pay for an education they would otherwise not be able to afford and, as a result, permit them to play a more significant role in society than might otherwise have been the case. There has always, therefore, been a mixture of rewarding talent and achievement, of providing an opportunity, and of expecting a return.

Nowadays the public purse is the major provider of funding for higher education and education itself has become a universal right in modern society. But, particularly at the university level, there is still need for support from patrons in the public and private sectors, and from private individuals and families. And there remains an important role for charitable foundations and private philanthropists. Higher education is expensive, is to a large degree selective, and for those passing through successfully it confers long-term social and economic benefits. Since there are elements of exclusion, and no system of selection is perfect, scholarships play a major part in evening out unfairness, especially of class or of economic deprivation. Almost all scholarship programs, therefore, have at their core an ideal of removing barriers to higher education and of developing talent to the full.

A government or a company might pay for a student to study particular subjects at a particular level. Conditions might be attached to such an award, for example that a scholarship holder perform certain tasks or put in a number of years of specified service. This is a fairly simple and explicit form of contract between patron and client: I pay for your education, and you work for me for x years after you qualify. Both parties are beneficiaries of the arrangement, and the terms of engagement are clear from the start. Other programs may not be framed in so clear-cut form. The reasons for philanthropic action are rarely straightforward, and most famous scholarship programs have, or had, a particular purpose in addition to a neutral one of providing educational opportunity. They all usually have the mark of their benefactors upon them, even if certain themes recur or if the original purposes weaken with time and circumstance.

Cecil Rhodes left some of his money to enable young men from the colonies of the British Empire to go to Oxford (thereby "giving breadth to their views for their instruction in life and manners and for instilling into their minds the advantage to the Colonies as well as to the United Kingdom of the retention of the unity of the Empire"). He included young men from the United States in his benefaction "out of a desire to encourage and foster an appreciation of the advantages which I implicitly believe will result from the union of the English-speaking peoples throughout the world."

The Truman Scholarships, established to celebrate the life and work of the thirty-third president of the United States, are designed for those who will commit themselves to a life of public service (a definition that is quite widely drawn). The Fulbright mission is "to foster mutual understanding among nations through education and cultural exchange." Marshall Scholarships commemorate the "humane ideals of the European Recovery Program" and seek to bring to the United Kingdom "intellectually distinguished young Americans who will one day become leaders, opinion formers and decision-makers in their own country" in order to enable them "to gain an understanding and appreciation of the British way of life and British social and academic values; to encourage them to be ambassadors to the United Kingdom for their own way of life, and to establish long-lasting bridges and ties between the peoples of the United States and the United Kingdom, at a personal level [and] to raise the profile of the United Kingdom in the United States, particularly among its young people." Ford looks to enable "a diverse group of exceptional men and women from many parts of the world, who would otherwise lack opportunities for advanced study, to pursue post-baccalaureate degrees." The Gates Foundation had two clear objectives in establishing the Gates Cambridge Trust: to create a "global scholarship program at Cambridge University which will attract the most academically talented graduate students from every country [and] to build a strong and influential alumni network of Gates Scholars around the world who will become future leaders." The list is endless, and the variations on theme and eligibility play one upon the other.

Faced with such a range of possibilities, those advising students about scholarship opportunities not surprisingly sometimes find it difficult to give the best advice. The problem may have become more intense in recent years partly because the number of good candidates far outstrips the number of scholarships available so competition for them has become that much greater, and partly because people get carried away by the high-flown rhetoric of good intention attached to most of these programs. They start to think that winning a scholarship is an end in itself, a mark of achievement, a complete reward. Universities and colleges boast that they have won so many of this or that award, and faculty members are put under pressure to achieve more and better results. More seriously, students themselves begin to think that winning a scholarship means they are at the top of the ladder rather than being given an opportunity to climb it; a process designed to help people become valued citizens and leaders tends to be one whereby distinction is bestowed prematurely, before the real work is done. Thus the delicate relationship between reward, opportunity, and obligation is thrown out of balance.

The responsible advice, as always, is to consider very carefully where the strengths of the students lie: what have they achieved, where is there further potential for growth. What sort of further education is really appropriate for them that will not only enrich them personally, but also help them to contribute to society in the best possible way? They may well be excellent candidates for some scholarships and not for others. The following questions, which relate to the particular scholarship program for which I have a responsibility, can be adapted easily to find a fit between aspiring student and appropriate scholarship. If they try for a Gates, do they really want to come to Cambridge? If they really want to come to Cambridge, are they coming for something that Cambridge not only does, but does well? Do they have the necessary qualifications to embark on the course for which they will apply? Does time spent at Cambridge fit sensibly into their considered plans? Will they take seriously a commitment to use the advantages which a Gates Cambridge Scholarship provides to, as Bill Gates puts it," bring new vision and apply their learning to the benefit of society at large?"

Well-educated young people are our investment in the future. In earlier centuries, royal and clerical patronage allowed universities quite pragmatically to educate bright boys for service in church and state. Now, governments, the private sector, and philanthropists the world over seek to reward those with potential by giving them opportunities for personal development that will enable them better to meet obligations to the wider community. When awarding scholarships, reward, yes, but do so on the basis of potential, selecting those who will have the opportunity to move forward to greater things, and who will feel an obligation to use the skills and talents thus developed to the best possible purposes.

7

Are You Comfortable Making the Call?

MARY HALE TOLAR

Mary Hale Tolar, a Truman Scholar (1988) and a Rhodes Scholar (Kansas and Lincoln, 1990), is the newly appointed executive director of Kansas Campus Compact at Kansas State University. She has established and directed post-graduate scholarship programs at The University of Tulsa and Willamette University, and worked closely with the scholarship program at George Washington University. In early 1999, she began serving as the deputy executive secretary of the Truman Scholarship Foundation and was the first to suggest the possibility of an organization that would have as its membership post-graduate scholarship advisors. She is a founding member of NAFA and was its inaugural foundation liaison.

In an Italian *frati* overlooking Lake Como, individuals charged with identifying and endowing the world's future leaders through competitive scholarships gathered to discuss the moral responsibility of our work. It was a great time. That was November of 2002, and that conference brought about not only lively, critical discussions and lasting, productive friendships, but also the report, "Strengthening Nationally Competitive Scholarships: Thoughts from an International Conference in Bellagio" found in this collection.

It also got me thinking. If there is a moral responsibility of scholarship programs to choose well, is there also a moral responsibility of scholarship advisors? And if so, what is it? What follows does not answer those questions; rather, it is an invitation to consider and respond to the moral implications of this work.

We might first grapple with the idea that scholarship advisors may have an identifiable moral responsibility. If the scholarship process is a worthwhile educational venture, and I have always argued that it is, would the moral responsibility of a scholarship advisor be the same or similar to the moral responsibility of an educator? Is the moral responsibility of advisors in some way unique? Does the scholarship process offer a unique opportunity, or apply to a unique audience? Does scholarship advising reflect a set of pedagogical techniques similar to or different from those of the classroom?

I would argue there is overlap, at the very least. I wonder, though, if the use or promotion of campus learning opportunities such as lecture series, cultural and arts events, extra- and co-curricular activities that allow students to explore their creativity, capacity for leadership, their power as citizens, and their future lives, might qualify as a kind of *campus,* as separate from classroom, *pedagogy.* It is nothing groundbreaking; it is college life outside the classroom. The idea has been around for awhile. But as scholarship advisors, we promote these "techniques" as a way to intentionally lead candidates through the scholarship process. The students we work with cannot simply accumulate sufficient credits for graduation; they must ask themselves hard questions and make connections between the courses they take, how they spend their time, and what they care about. Life outside the classroom weighs in heavily to this process. It is both a testing ground for students, which is critical to personal development, and evidence of their commitment to articulated ideas and values, which is most helpful to scholarship selectors.

Our moral responsibility may well be linked to that of the educator. Is it also related in some way to that of the scholarship programs? If the moral (or perhaps social?) responsibility of the scholarship programs is to bestow the accumulation of advantage on the worthy, how does that translate into a moral responsibility of the advisor? Might one ask how do I as an advisor confer accumulation of advantage to students on my own campus? These are merit-based competitions. How true are my, or my institution's, means of distinguishing merit?

How we run campus selection and advising processes matters—to the student, to the institution, and to the scholarship program. Are we modeling good *and* bad practices inherited from scholarship programs, in an effort to give our students the greatest opportunity for success at the next level? Is there an inherent conflict when higher education aims (perhaps arguably) to be as inclusive as possible, whereas scholarship programs, at least on the surface, do not? Ah, the familiar "elitism" tension. But a critical piece of our moral responsibility must be how we work within the university to serve the mission of our institution.

Tension is no stranger to scholarship advisors. We serve our students, our institutions, and the scholarship programs. Our responsibility to each at times conflicts with the others. Helping a bright, gifted student come to understand that she does not wish to compete for a Rhodes is satisfying on the one hand—she is on her way to build the life she chooses—and hard to take on the other—she was the most competitive candidate that has come through your institution in a long while. Or you promote a candidate who will help bring energy and visibility to the campus scholarship program, and will certainly grow from the process (and may even win), but who is not the best match for the program—you have reason to believe that this Truman candidate is likely to end up in the private sector, perhaps. How we deal with this tension matters to students, our institutions, and scholarship programs. It matters to us personally and to our profession.

This tension put bluntly becomes the question that makes us squirm: How do we deal with the understanding that the more skilled the advisor, the more likely a candidate is to advance without cause? One way we are dealing with that is through participation in National Association of Fellowships Advisors, and its commitment to explore, and make clear, standards of ethical conduct. We have a responsibility to be ethical in our representation to students and to programs. Through discussions, debate, shared experiences, and collective wisdom, we will develop and make good use of these guideposts, establishing a code of ethics for NAFA members.

But there is another consideration. Do we, in our capacity as moral scholarship advisors, get to determine the "good," not just competitive, candidates? Do we have a personal, moral responsibility to promote our own world view? Sticky, eh?

When I first started serving on selection panels, I was a little uncomfortable. After all, I had been a scholarship advisor for a long time. I had known many exceptional students who had been passed over by committees, and a few mediocre or even questionable ones who succeeded. Would I be able to see what I needed to in order to choose wisely? If a candidate struck a wrong chord with me, the problem could well be with me, couldn't it? What if I had an off day? Not enough coffee. Too much. And really, do I have to like the person, or what he stands for, for him to qualify for a scholarship?

These questions were not new, of course. Every year when it came time to nominate candidates from campus I would go through this. But the difference now was that there was no "next level," as in, "they'll catch it at the next level." If scholarship advisors truly comprise the first vetting of the world's future leaders, don't they then have a moral responsibility to promote students who they believe will lead well? Not just effectively, but well. (This is the well-worn leadership question: Was Hitler a good leader?)

Still, who am I to make these judgments?

I have gone along with selection committees on choices I disagreed with, primarily because I believe in the process and respect my fellow committee members. And I do think the process works. But there are two or three who stand out, candidates who added up in all measurable respects, truly defensible choices, who I knew were not good choices. My gut said no. Early on, I kept my gut out of it, for all the reasons I mention above. Eventually I learned to trust myself, and gave myself permission to pass judgment—moral judgment. The questionable few, the ones who view scholarships as personal social advancement, make it through and do accumulate advantage. They gain access. They become leaders. I may not always be comfortable making the call. And there is good reason for a committee process. One person's opinion is never the final say. But ultimately, if not me, if not us, who?

As NAFA considers its code of ethics, and as we continue to convene, discuss, and share our work—the challenges and the rewards—these questions of moral responsibility will continue to surface. Scholarship advisors serve students, institutions, and scholarship programs with that inherent tension. How can we avoid these questions? And who wants to? Tension can produce remarkable change. It is not always comfortable, but working together to explore our roles and responsibilities better prepares us for making the call. Now, if we could only continue this conversation overlooking Lake Como. . . .

8

Elocution Lessons?

An Ethical Approach to Advising

SUZANNE D. McCRAY

Suzanne D. McCray, the associate dean of the Honors College at the University of Arkansas, also directs the Office of Post-Graduate Fellowships and regularly teaches honors seminars. Before joining the University of Arkansas, she served as a co-director of the Anglo-American Library at the University of Cluj in Cluj-Napoca, Romania. She began scholarship advising at Arkansas as part of her honors responsibilities in 1992, creating the Office of Post-Graduate Fellowships in 1998. She has served as vice president and president (2003–5) of the National Association of Fellowship Advisors.

The members of NAFA have made clear that the process of applying for competitive scholarships and grants provides the most important outcome for students. They learn about themselves, about what they want to do, and about what they may want to become. Applying for scholarships can help a student develop good habits—reading widely, examining assumptions, getting organized early, proofreading carefully—that can last a lifetime.

Many of us also connect with students in ways beyond advising them on scholarships. Our positions expand the process to include teaching or undergraduate research. Many of us mentor students early in their academic careers before we have a sense of whether or not the student can or will want to apply for scholarships. All of us spend hours working with applicants who do not seem as competitive as others because we can see an immediate benefit. But such a process does not always make good copy for our institutions or for a public trying to understand what it is we do. It can, at times, seem like a justification for not winning.

NAFA was already attracting national attention as we met at our first conference in Tulsa, Oklahoma, in 2001. Andy Brownstein from the *Chronicle of Higher Education* attended that conference, trying to understand what we do. He spoke to a variety of people, participated on the NAFA listserv briefly, and visited Oklahoma State University repeatedly. He, too, wanted to get it right, and the article he ultimately wrote was a fair portrait. But some of the questions he asked indicated that he was focused on the competition more than the process. He asked one question that made me take a second look. He asked me, as an advisor in a rural state, if we provide elocution lessons for our students. I was surprised both about the assumption of need and the implied suggestion that we would should that need arise, and told him absolutely not. He noted my somewhat surprised tone and pointed to the practice interviews, the practice social events. Why not lessons? What's the difference? For me, there is a fundamental difference that gets at the heart of the matter.

We do not try to change who our students are. We practice to help students relax, to become familiar with interview situations, to respond thoughtfully, to engage in ideas, and to be comfortable when those ideas are challenged. But we would/should never do anything to indicate to students that we do not find them acceptable people. Arkansas—and other university—students are from a variety of places, with a variety of accents, and surely being from a place or having a background different from the norm can be interesting.

Mike Winerip of the *New York Times* wrote a January 2003 feature that once again focused on scholarship advising. His focus was restricted to one scholarship, his contacts were more limited, and his visits centered on practice interviews. Specific advice given to specific students when asked specific questions sounded like prescriptions for winning—wear pantsuits, drink at the cocktail party, read the following. We all know that such prescriptions do not work. A robust, engaged student who is likely to receive a competitive scholarship is not one who can be mass produced. None of us imagine it possible. The article was right on the mark, however, when it reported that students do not "naturally" apply for these scholarships. They need reliable information, good advice, and collegial support. That's why NAFA exists.

Ethical Advising

Ethical questions interest me very much, but I am not a philosopher and cannot provide a systematic understanding of our ethical mission[1]. My degrees are in literature, and certainly there are relevant ethical lessons to be drawn there. Hector's moving speech to Andromache in Book Six of the *Iliad* is a wonderful treatise on the rewards of losing the right way, while Wiglaf's fierce castigation of the cowardly warriors in *Beowulf* warns us that winning the wrong way has costs too enormous to be borne. These are lessons our own lives teach us to know and understand—glorious defeat and inglorious victory. We do not long for either.

Members of NAFA are honorable people guiding honorable students though the scholarship application process. So why NAFA's intense focus on ethics? Perhaps it is because the ethical situations we face do not quite so neatly sort themselves out as they do for Hector and for Wiglaf. Ours is not the heroic world, though we deal regularly with victories and defeats, and the work we do has important consequences. We interact with students who are for the most part young, facing important moments in their lives, and looking to us for direction. They come to us for help in evaluating and interpreting their past achievements, for advice on their present activities, and for a sense of the impact both will have on their future opportunities. And we want to get it as right as we can.

To do this we need to first ask questions that will help unlock a variety of doors, not just the doors our institutions can recognize and can count. To get it right, to interact with students in ways that are most beneficial to them and finally most rewarding to us, we have to examine and reexamine what we do and how we do it. Continuing to examine ourselves and to share these questions with each other as new and ever complex situations arise is one of the best ways to do that. Members of NAFA are asking questions, and we are asking them on a daily basis. I sent out a message on the listserv requesting examples of the questions advisors ask and compiled pages of both general and school-specific concerns. The question most felt was being asked by upper administration was "Isn't winning everything?" The questions advisors really want to hear are "How else do students benefit from coming to your office?" and "Are we asking you to do more than you can do and do it well and fairly for all your students?" By "fairly" here I just mean giving all the students who come in the door the time they need.

Other important institutional questions for us come when our students do win. How do we celebrate their achievements in ways that make them feel appreciated and honored, and not like their accomplishments are reduced to recruiting or development tools? When we share our records with high school students, their parents, and their counselors—and we do share—then we must make good on everything that record implies. We must continue to provide and develop exciting and challenging course work, opportunities for undergraduate research, funding for special academic and study abroad opportunities, as well as the commitment to provide informed assistance through the scholarship application process.

While these institutional concerns are very important to us, the heart of what we do occurs across the table from a student. The bulk of ethical questions that have been generated on the listserv and at various conferences arise from those interactions. We have institutional concerns, but questions connected with students become worries. I am by nature a worrier, and directing a fellowships office has given professional sanction to that habit. What are some of our worries? The most basic is that we give informed, sound advice. When we hang a shingle outside our door that says (I'll use my office title as an example) "Office of Post-Graduate Fellowships," we promise just that. It is a serious responsibility, and so we have

NAFA, a venue to exchanges ideas, to keep current, to ask questions, so we can make good on our promise.

My life as a scholarship advisor had an inauspicious beginning. Our campus wanted to jump start the number of students applying for the Barry Goldwater and Truman Scholarships. This was 1992 and I had been a program coordinator in honors for two years. We did not have much of a system in place—faculty scholarship representatives were scattered across the campus. There was no coordinated effort, no committees, no mock interviews, no real assistance. But in 1992 the effort was more coordinated. We had three viable candidates. I was so eager to do it right that I mailed the applications a week ahead of the deadline (the only time in my career that has happened). I felt great until two days before the deadline when a call came from a college of engineering assistant dean letting me know that engineering had two candidates for the Barry Goldwater Scholarship. I reported that the applications for three students had already been mailed and which of the two would he like to put forward. He told me he was putting forward both and that we must withdraw one of the other students since all three came from the college of arts and sciences.

That was when I learned that there was a standing agreement between arts and sciences and engineering that each could put forward two candidates. I asked if that agreement stood regardless of the students' qualifications. I learned it did. I called the Barry Goldwater Scholarship and pulled our sophomore applicant, thinking we could put her forward again the following year. I waited to send these two new applications that I had not yet seen. When I did finally get them, it was clear that one of the students did not qualify. I Fedexed the qualified application and called the Barry Goldwater Scholarship Office again to ask if it would be possible to reinstate our sophomore. They allowed it, and the obvious ending to this story is that she won. This was the best thing that could have happened from the point of reorganizing our process. To take a line from the sometimes-ethical Mick Jagger, "You can't always get what you want, but sometimes you get what you need."

No one argued the next year when we put together a committee of scientists, set a campus deadline, and did away with this artificial right to applicants. The next year, three of our students received Barry Goldwater Scholarships. This was compelling evidence to us that it was time to get equally organized with other scholarships as well, and to address how nominees were selected. Many advisors have the same worries on their campuses. That we are asking questions means that as we form committees in the future we will be more acutely aware of possible conflicts of interest and solve some of the problems before they begin. Asking and resolving go hand in hand.

The question that always looms large for the scholarship advisor is how much help is too much? I do not tend to worry much about the pragmatic end of that question. I mark students' essays like I would in a composition class. I mark errors, question word choices, ask for explanations, draw arrows, circle repeated words, especially the excessive use of "I." I don't write sentences, but I do mark several drafts. We have a writing center that has an ethical guide for assisting with student papers, and we follow it in my office. It works well for us. I worry more about the less concrete side of that question. I worry about the language we use when advising students. Saying that internship sounds great and will really look good on a Truman application is tempting, but unwise. We want to support passions, not nurture a "Habitat for Scholarships" culture. If we do this we are helping too much. If we listen to their dreams and try to shape them to fit a scholarship, we are helping too much. If we advise them to play it safe in their course work to keep grades high, we are helping too much.

My first experience with giving advice on a scholarship occurred close to home before I started working in honors. My husband was applying for a Guggenheim Fellowship and asked my take on his personal statement. In it he mentioned that he had been fired early in his career from his first university teaching position for violations of the dress code. His sartorial style was and is simple—T-shirts and shorts or jeans for teaching, a shirt with a collar for special occasions. His chair sent a letter asking him to revise this style. He posted the letter to his door, rented and wore a tux for a week, and was promptly fired. This is actually a very telling story about him, but my advice was that including it might be off-putting to a committee. They might misread it, finding him more arrogant than amusing. It seemed risky.

Helen Mann, vice consul for the British Consulate General in Houston, says "You want to get the committee by the throat." I wondered if his grip might be too tight. It was the only part of the application he worried about, but finally he decided the entire application was risky—the odds were against him—and why not go down saying what you want to say when you are probably going to go down any way? So he said what he wanted to, and he received the fellowship. That fellowship is different, of course, in its expectations than the ones we work with, but I often think of it when I am advising students. It reminds me that risks are often good things. While students can ask for our takes on their essays, the students must worry as well, and the students are the ones who must decide. Applying for scholarships is a risky business in general. Students risk the most. They do the endless hours of writing and rewriting. They listen to suggestions that they may feel are unnecessarily critical. They face the possibility of rejection on their campus, or at the foundation level. And it feels personal because they have put much of themselves on the page. Most students decide it is a risk worth taking. You can't always get what you want, but sometimes you get what you need. And of course, there are those wonderful moments when you get both.

9

The Rhodes to Perdition

Mapping A Detour Around Professional Potholes

DON ANDREW

Don Andrew directs the fellowships program at Smith College, which he established in 2001. Formerly a political and financial journalist and writer, he has worked in a dozen countries. He served with the late David Dellinger on the board of Toward Freedom, a thirty-five-year-old periodic report on the nonaligned movement. Active in the antiapartheid movement, he orchestrated a press and Parliamentary exposé of international fraud and propagandistic corruption: the "Info Scandal" unseated the regime of prime minister John Vorster, breaking its stranglehold on South Africa. The resistance movement rose to fill the vacuum, apartheid began to crumble and a decade later Nelson Mandela was freed.

"**F**our!" the college president intoned his mantra reserved for me as he held up four fingers every time our paths crossed. "Four Goldwaters. I want four Goldwaters!"

Possessed as he was by this specific prize, the process involved in applying and competing for fellowships didn't occur to him, a mad scientist with a funny fellowships fetish and fixation on four. My performance was judged purely by the prizes I produced, particularly, or should I say, peculiarly in his case, the Goldwater.

After we had won his famous four, or should I say, after OUR STUDENTS HAD WON four Goldwaters, he said to me: "So do you get to keep your job?"

Nice, isn't it? This story was told to me by a fellow fellowships advisor. Yes, our job, as delightful as it is to advise exceptional students at our institutions, is, at the end of the day, no matter what is said to the contrary, judged by the number of winners we bring so our colleges can brag. For good reason, too—winning attracts better students and faculty, and helps raise money.

But we know the ultimate prize of winning is only half the prize. The other half comprises the benefits of the process to the student. So it should be if we are managing to do our jobs decently and resisting pressure to produce winners regardless of whether the process is beneficial to the applicants. It is great to win. But at what cost? This dilemma goes straight to the heart of what defines our profession of fellowships advising.

The Denver conference theme "Beyond Winning" ties to articles that have appeared in the *New York Times* ("Fellowship of the Rhodes," January 12, 2003) and in the *Chronicle of Higher Education* ("Ambitious Colleges End the Ivy Lock on Prestigious Fellowships," September 2001). Both articles raised contentious issues about our profession that, like this year's conference, address the process of applying and preparing for fellowship competitions.

The conference will seek to show that not only should the end (winning) justify the means (competing), the means (process) should be an end in itself. The contentious issue at stake is over some of the means we might be tempted to employ in order to satisfy college expectations, implicit or explicit, even outright demands. There is no getting away from the fact that our job performance is judged *inter alia* by the number of winners we produce.

Let us reflect upon the question of grooming (scouting, recruiting, mentoring, advising, coaching, prepping, rehearsing) in order to reconcile any conflicting approaches to our profession so that we can advance our common goals. Both articles sought to some degree (even to the third) to spotlight or sensationalize the lengths to which colleges can go to win, to the extent that this smacked of fellowships engineering. Our profession as a whole was tainted by some of the insinuations. Yet we are wise enough to simply and calmly see what we can learn from this by the same self-searching we expect from the fellowship aspirants who come knocking at our doors. Or as one colleague put it regarding the more eager variety, those panting at her door.

Let us bind together to grapple with the core issues raised—touchy, ticklish, and tricky as they are—that still confront us, and indeed are the shadow image of the conference theme.

There is a point at which the end of winning no longer justifies the means, hence the need to ensure the benefits of the process are as worthy as the prize, that the means themselves justify even the pursuit of the ends. In other words, it is not so much a matter of the lengths to which some colleges go or must go to win, but rather a question of applying the acid test whether these lengths are themselves educational and beneficial to the fellowship applicants.

If not, then we might say there is a danger of traveling "the Rhodes to Perdition" should the prize mentality become an obsession riding rough-shod over a justifiable process. If the process itself of rewriting an essay over and over and practicing at multiple mock interviews does not benefit the student beyond winning, then the end does not justify the means. There can be a fine line between guiding a star to a self-fulfilling fellow-ship, and reshaping less-promising students (and their applications) into fellows.

A keen young fellowships prospect in our college's top one percent asked me recently if she should give up her position on the varsity swim team since this took up so much time that she could devote to volunteer-ing. The rest of her spare time is spent in a lab as a research assistant to a professor. I counseled her to honor her athleticism and keep swimming. I feel morally obliged to advise students to remain true to themselves. However much I might feel tempted that she has the makings to be our first American Rhodes Scholar, I am not prepared to advise she change her life for the sole purpose of winning. Not that volunteering is necessarily better than swimming for the Rhodes, but I do not want to create fellowship winners like some test-tube baby. I want only to bring out the American Rhodes Scholar (if only I could find one!) that is already within a student.

Yes, as trite as it may sound, life is bigger than the Rhodes. The problem is the *New York Times* article made it sound that winning was pursued at all costs, so to speak, or at least at great cost, even when it was unclear that the cost was worth it to the students, regardless of the prize. It painted a picture of self-flagellation almost, amid a whipped-up frenzy of bewildered losers crushed after a marathon. As Yale fellowships advisor Mark Bauer commented on our listserv after the *Times* article appeared: "It gets a lot wrong about fellowship advising and, by extension, NAFA's mission and philosophy."

Again, despite the article's inaccuracies, while we face prize pressure, the issue of grooming remains. The *Chronicle* went so far as to "expose" an unnamed college's "secret formula" for pumping out Trumans, Marshalls, Goldwaters, and so on that essentially relied on an advisor micromanaging all aspects of the applications to the point of instructing applicants what to write, resulting in insincere essay self-portrayals. Call them betrayals.

At my college, I have been reciting my own mantra from my soapbox: "There are no losers in our fellowships program. All emerge winners from the enriching process." Fortunately, my superiors see the virtue in this holistic embrace. Nevertheless, it takes a lot to beat a headline boasting major fellowship wins. It is a hallowed knighting with a glittering sword that few other single events can bestow on a college and its extended community in one swift, stark stroke to boost its pride and prestige.

See how easy it is to forget the students as we get caught up in the glory? As least as much as we use them for the fame and fortune of the college, should we ensure that their best interests come first? We can never be too vigilant about this. And we can all do with reminding about it.

The ultimate test is this: If the student does not win, and most do not, then was the process itself still profoundly worth it for the student? It will usually be found that the bigger the benefit of the process to the student, the less the disappointment experienced at not winning.

It does not serve our students for us to have such an eye on the prize that the future supersedes the present because then the greatest gift yielded by the process will be too elusive. The deepest benefit from the fellowships application and preparation process, besides obvious skills acquisition, is its potential of being an initiation into adulthood through a process of self-reflection and self-discovery that leads to a higher degree of the practical philosophical treasure that is self-knowledge.

This becomes even more important if we take seriously a more recent *Chronicle* article that proclaimed the fellowships system is in the business of choosing tomorrow's leaders. If we want to place the future of our planet in wise hands, then we are duty-bound to ensure our applicants have applied the perennial dictum know thyself.

Leaders driven by impulses of which they are unaware are perilous. Leaders in whom lurk hidden motives are treacherous. It is a tragedy how some bad leaders stay in power so long to wreak so much harm and hurt so many. It is a reflection of a society for which its citizens are responsible when callous politicians masquerading behind masks of compassion end up in power.

As much as we groom, let us do our part to weed out those who do not convincingly demonstrate good character. Let us ensure we truly and thoroughly know those whom we endorse, nominate, and otherwise sponsor. Let us truly take to heart "who" the foundations say they seek: those with a vision, and the talent and motivation to serve humankind in order to improve society. The globe has shrunk and with it power continues to concentrate in fewer hands. The potential to do good or harm has multiplied, especially for powerful nations.

Let us have the courage to state honestly any unavoidable character reservations we have about those whose applications we forward, even if it means forfeiting a fellowship. We had a candidate in a competition who was marked down on the evaluation rating because of concerns about character issues involving reliability, conscientiousness, and candor, as she went about producing application materials for the various campus screening stages. Our comments about this on the foundation form may have cost an otherwise outstanding candidate the fellowship as she was named an alternate.

Perhaps we will each need to put fewer applicants into the pipeline, only those who in our heart of hearts we believe deserve the fellowship, and will make excellent fellows, and who genuinely stand an above-average chance of winning. The foundations are bound to force this in time with new restrictions to up the ante, for instance by raising the eligibility bar. This has already happened with the Rhodes's academic standards, and the Marshall has shifted away from the humanities. Another step to shrinking the pool might be to limit the number of "nominees" per institution, as with the Truman and Udall except that could limit the foundations' options in finding the very best nationally (as the Fulbright and Gates strive to achieve) if state representation is not part of their objective. Regional competition pools tend to be complex and uneven or seem less straightforward and more inscrutable—not that regional competitions themselves put a cap on institutional participation.

As it is, the fellowship competitions are being swamped (just witness the spectacular rise in Fulbright applications last year, for instance) and may become clogged. While NAFA strives for high standards, we equally popularize more participation. We are creating more competition for ourselves even as we help each other. This is healthy, but it does demand that we each raise our own standards, intrinsically, rather than concentrating overly on the outward push for the prize.

If we roll out Rhodes robots and manufacture Marshall machines, we have failed. The process must not turn students into who they are not, but rather make the inherently worthy more who they are. Then we all win the Self-Fulfillment Fellowship.

10

Strengthening Nationally Competitive Scholarships

Thoughts from an International Conference in Bellagio

ALICE STONE ILCHMAN, WARREN F. ILCHMAN, AND MARY HALE TOLAR

Alice Ilchman is the director of the Jeannette K. Watson Fellowships of the Thomas Watson Foundation. She served as president of Sarah Lawrence College for seventeen years beginning in 1981. Prior to her appointment as president, Ilchman served as assistant secretary for education and cultural affairs in the Department of State during the Carter administration. She is also currently the chair of the board of trustees of the Rockefeller Foundation.

Warren Ilchman is director of the Paul and Daisy Soros Foundation. He has been on the faculty or administered at Williams College, University of

California at Berkeley, Boston University, State University of New York at Albany, Pratt Institute, and Indiana University. He was also a staff member of the Ford Foundation. He is the author or editor of fourteen books including The Political Economy of Change *(1998) and* The Lucky Few and the Worthy Many: Scholarship Competitions and the World's Future Leaders *(2004).*

Mary Hale Tolar, a Truman Scholar (1988) and a Rhodes Scholar (1989), is the newly appointed executive director of Kansas Campus Compact. She has established and directed post-graduate scholarship programs at The University of Tulsa and Willamette University, and worked closely with the scholarship program at George Washington University. In early 1999, she began serving as the deputy executive secretary of the Truman Scholarship Foundation and was the first to suggest the possibility of an organization that would have as its membership post-graduate scholarship advisors. She is a founding member of NAFA and was its inaugural foundation liaison.

Why This Is Important to Us

Among those who convened in Bellagio, much was shared in common.[1] Our respective missions in managing nationally competitive scholarships aim at enhancing the potential of young people to lead more useful and creative lives, both for themselves and for others. Programs like many of those featured at Bellagio are international in character (both in terms of the origins of candidates and their academic destinations), and are needed now more than ever to build a world of mutual understanding and shared values. Finally, our programs advance the acquisition of skills important to building better societies. What we can share that helps us in our appointed work also rebounds to the advantage of successive generations. We don't believe that there is better work.

The authors were particularly drawn to the subject of strengthening nationally competitive scholarships for three reasons. First, as individuals charged with producing results wished by donors—whether philanthropic or government—we want to know what constitutes "good evidence" that we have been successful in our missions, that we have exercised due diligence in discharging our responsibilities, and we want to have these answers in good time to improve our process and outcomes. Second, as people responsible for such scholarships, we are concerned about how to choose the lucky few from among the worthy many. Our task in practice becomes finding grounds for rejecting applicants rather than for their selection, as there are so many individuals qualified and capable to fulfill the objectives of our programs. Surely, we think, there must be positive measures to take that would discern "worthiness" better. And, finally, given the amount of experience in managing such programs among those at Bellagio, there must be better ways to organize panels, conduct interviews, and add value to the fellowship for our finalists. From our collective experience, there should be standards that will assist us all.

There is an additional concern of ours, born of a commitment to equity and productivity. As citizens in societies concerned with merit, we believe that talent is broadly, even randomly, distributed, but only selectively developed. Because many able, talented people have not had the privilege of selective development—experiences that make candidates more attractive and available to those who select them—we are concerned that we may be missing many qualified individuals, often from groups underrepresented in many ways in our societies. Missing their potential contributions deprives not only them but all of us. It seems worthwhile to enlarge the pool even at the expense of having more disappointed people—those worthy but unchosen many.

There is an additional dimension of fairness that concerns us. While no economist has estimated what difference the possession of a Rhodes or similar scholarship means in terms of a lifetime's income, we assume that it is substantial. More particularly, by anecdotes and experience, we have noted in recipients of scholarships what Harriet Zuckerman calls the "accumulation of advantage," where receiving one scholarship leads to other forms of support in critical periods of building a career.[2] This has been called in science the Matthew Effect.[3] In addition, based on the work of Pierre Bourdieu, we noted how scholarship programs tend to reproduce certain characteristics of dominant groups in their recipients, how finalists tend to look like, talk like, and value what we find in the programs' panelists.[4] Within the twin commitments to merit and equity, how have various scholarship programs addressed these concerns?

The Universe of Nationally Competitive Scholarships

Nationally competitive scholarships have long been a tool used by foundations and governments to advance the acquisition of critical skills, further the goals of citizenship, nurture creativity, and develop the qualities of leadership. After a very long history (in one case nearly a century) of scholarship competitions, three major new fellowships have been launched. The Ford Foundation inaugurated in 2000 a program of $280 million, the largest grant in its history, to support graduate study anywhere in the world. The goal is to fund within ten years 3,500 individuals from Africa, Asia, and Latin America.[5] A major new undertaking is the endowment of $210 million from the Bill and Melinda Gates Foundation to the University of Cambridge. When this program is in full operation, the Gates Cambridge Trust expects to support 225 students from around the world studying at the graduate level at Cambridge in fields that relate to such global problems as health equity, technology, and learning. Finally, within the last decade, the Open Society Institute (George Soros's philanthropic organization) has established many graduate competitive scholarship programs for Central and Eastern Europe and Central Asia, as well as for Burma and Africa. Approximately one thousand scholarships are awarded annually among thirty countries.

These dramatic new efforts at nationally competitive scholarships join a field of well-established programs with long experience in both managing domestic and international scholarship programs. Originating from Europe, there are many, including the oldest, the Rhodes Trust. The German DAAD (Deutsche Akademischer Austauschdienst), the Erasmus/Socrates programs of the European Union, the Commonwealth Scholars program of the Association of Commonwealth Universities, the British Marshall Fund, and the many programs associated with the Academic Cooperative Association involve significant numbers of students in their scholarly exchanges to acquire critical skills, nurture creativity, further goals of citizenship and mobility among university students, and develop leadership as their objectives.

Apart from the Erasmus/Socrates program of the European Union, the DAAD may be the largest scholarship-awarding program in the world. For its undergraduate and graduate scholarship and related programs in 2000, grants were made to 14,687 Germans to study outside of Germany and for 21,334 non-Germans to study in Germany.[6]

For the United States, such long-standing programs come to mind as the Fulbright, the Woodrow Wilson National Fellowship Foundation, the Luce Scholars, the Hertz Fellowships, the Mellon Humanities Fellowships, the Howard Hughes Fellowships, the Truman Scholarships, and the Thomas J. Watson Fellowships. In addition there are competitive graduate fellowships sponsored by the United States government through the National Science Foundation and the National Institutes of Health.

In United States–related programs alone, there are an estimated six thousand nationally competitive scholarships annually (not including those offered by the universities themselves), with an annual direct cost of one hundred million dollars. Many of these scholarships are multiple-year in duration (Howard Hughes, Hertz, National Science Foundation, etc.) and, conservatively estimated, probably bring the direct expenditure annually for United States residents to over four hundred million dollars.

To get a grasp on the variety and size of the principal programs, we offer the following taxonomy (Table 1).

Commonalities and Differences in Scholarship Programs

SCHOLARSHIP OBJECTIVES

An important point of departure is what the scholarships wish to achieve and who they believe can best achieve it. A classic statement is the one contained in the 1901 will of Cecil Rhodes establishing the Rhodes Scholarships. To foster and encourage an appreciation of the advantages of the union of English-speaking peoples throughout the world, his will identified four criteria for selection:

> My desire being that the students who shall be elected to the Scholarships shall not be merely bookworms I direct that in the election of a student to a Scholarship regard shall be had to (i) his literary and scholastic attainments (ii) his fondness of and success in manly outdoor sports such as cricket football and the like (iii) his qualities of manhood

TABLE 1: TAXONOMY OF SELECTED NATIONALLY COMPETITIVE SCHOLARSHIPS

Fellowship	Founded	Source of Funds	No. of Applicants (approx.)	No. of Awards	Duration	Award Value (max.)*	Selection Process	Institutional Endorsement	Origin	Destination
Beinecke Scholarships	1971	Private foundation	100	20	5 years	$32,000	Delegated	Yes; invited institutions only	US	US or international
Churchill Scholarships	1959	Private foundation	150	11	1 year	$27,000	Delegated	Yes; invited institutions only	US	UK
Commonwealth Scholarship and Fellowship Plan—General Scholarships	1959	Government	N/A	N/A	Up to 3 years	TF, M, B, E, Tr, F	Delegated	Varies by country	Commonwealth Countries	UK
Jack Kent Cooke Graduate Scholarships	1997	Private foundation	675	50	2 years	$60,000	Delegated	Yes	US	Not stated
DAAD Deutschlandjahr Scholarships for Graduating Seniors	1971	Government	200–250	150–200	1 academic year	$6,650; B, Tr, I	Delegated	Yes	US, Canada	Germany
European Commission Erasmus/Socrates Program	1987	Government	N/A	N/A	1 semester, 1 year	Varies by country	Delegated	Yes	EU	EU
Ford Foundation International Fellowships Program (IFP)	2000	Private foundation	N/A	Varies; 95 in 2000, 557 by end of 2002	3 years	T, M, Tr, F	Delegated	No	21 IFP countries (Africa, Asia, L. America, Middle East, Eastern Europe)	Europe, Russia, US, L. America, Canada, Africa, Asia, Australia

TABLE I continued

Fellowship	Founded	Source of Funds	No. of Applicants (approx.)	No. of Awards	Duration	Award Value (max.)*	Selection Process	Institutional Endorsement	Origin	Destination
Fulbright Program–Incoming Student Program	1946	Government(s)	N/A	2,200+	1 academic year (plus renewals)	Full award: T, M, B, Tr, I. Varies by country	Direct	Yes; U.S. university admission required	140 countries	US
Fulbright Program–US Scholar Program	1946	Government(s)	4,000–5,000	1,000+	1 year (plus extensions, renewals)	T, M, B, Tr, I, L. Varies by country	Delegated and direct	Yes, but may also apply at-large	US	140 participating countries
Gates Cambridge Scholarships	2001	Private foundation	500	90	1 to 3 years	T, M, Tr	Direct and delegated	No	All countries except UK	UK
German Chancellor Scholarships/Humboldt Foundation	1990	Private foundation	N/A	10	1 year	M, B, L	Delegated	No	N. America	Germany
Hertz Foundation Graduate Fellowships	1963	Private foundation	500–700	25	5 years	$125,000; T	Direct	No; invited institutions only	US	US
Howard Hughes Medical Institute (HHMI)–Predoctoral Fellowships in Biological Science^	1988	Private foundation	1,100	80	5 years	$37,000/year	Delegated	No	US	US; abroad in some cases
HHMI/EMBO Young Investigators and Scientists^	2002	Private foundation	35	5	3 years	$30,000/year	Direct	No	Czech Republic, Hungary, Poland	Czech Republic, Hungary, Poland

TABLE I continued

Fellowship	Founded	Source of Funds	No. of Applicants (approx.)	No. of Awards	Duration	Award Value (max.)*	Selection Process	Institutional Endorsement	Origin	Destination
HHMI–Research Training Fellowships for Medical Students	1989	Private foundation	180	77	1 or 2 years	$37,000	Direct	No	US	US; abroad in some cases
HHMI/NIH Research Scholars	1985	Private foundation	170	42	1 or 2 years	$37,000	Direct	No	US	US
Kennedy Memorial Scholarships	1966	Private foundation	N/A	12	1 or 2 years	T, M, Tr, I	Direct	Yes	UK	US
Luce Scholars Program	1974	Private foundation	130	18	1 year	M, H	Direct and delegated	Yes; invited institutions only	US	Asia
MacArthur Fellows Program	1981	Private foundation	N/A	20–30	5 years	$500,000	Delegated	No; anonymous "nominators"	US	Not stated
Marshall Scholarships	1953	Government	800–900	Up to 40	2 or 3 years	T, F, M, r B, T	Delegated	Yes	US	UK
Mellon Fellowships in Humanistic Studies	1982	Private foundation	775	85	1 year	$17,500; T, F	Delegated	No	US	US or Canada
Mitchell Scholarships	1998	Government/ Private partnership	unavailable	12	1 year	$11,000; T, H, Tr	Delegated	Yes	US	Ireland and N. Ireland
National Science Foundation Graduate Research Fellowships	1952	Government	5,000–6,000	900	3 years, over 5-year period	$21,000; $10,000 to institution; $1,000 (Tr)	Delegated	No	US	US

TABLE I continued

Fellowship	Founded	Source of Funds	No. of Applicants (approx.)	No. of Awards	Duration	Award Value (max.)*	Selection Process	Institutional Endorsement	Origin	Destination
Open Society Institute Fellowships	1993	Private foundation, Government(s), University cost-share	8,000	1,000	1 year, some multiyear	$1,500 to $70,000; Varies by country	Direct and delegated	Yes	E. and C. Europe, Mongolia, former Soviet Union, Burma	US, UK, France, Germany, S.E. Asia, and countries of origin
Rhodes Scholarships	1904	Private foundation	N/A	94	2 or 3 years	T, M, Tr, F	Delegated	Yes	Commonwealth, US, Germany, and Hong Kong	UK
Rotary Ambassadorial Scholarships	1947	Private foundation	1,300	1,000	1 year	$25,000	Direct	No; by local Rotary club	100 Rotary countries	100 Rotary countries
Soros Fellowships	1997	Private foundation	1,000	30	Up to 2 years	$20,000/ year; T	Delegated	Yes	US	US
Truman Scholarships	1975	Government	600	75 to 80	4 years	$30,000	Delegated	Yes	US	US or international
Watson Fellowships	1968	Private foundation	180–190	Up to 60	1 year	$22,000; F	Direct	Yes	US	Varies; international

*Value stated in U.S. dollars. For those programs that do not provide award value in currency, the following key is used: T = Tuition, F = University fees, M = Maintenance/living expenses, H = Housing, B = Books/research expenses, E = Equipment, Tr = Travel, F = Family allowance, I = Health/accident insurance, L = Language course/tuition

^These grants have been suspended but were represented at the conference.

truth courage devotion to duty sympathy for and protection of the weak kindliness unselfishness and fellowship and (iv) his exhibition during school days of moral force of character and instincts to lead and to take an interest in his schoolmates for those latter attributes will be likely in afterlife to guide him to esteem the performance of public duties as his highest aim (punctuation—or lack of it—is in the original will).[7]

Several fellowship programs followed this model. The Commonwealth Fund in New York, for instance, created in 1924 a "reverse Rhodes" called Harkness Fellows with similar qualifications for students from Great Britain and the Commonwealth. When the Fulbright program was founded in 1946, Senator J. William Fulbright claimed lineage from his Rhodes experience. In many subsequent scholarship programs, the language of the Rhodes will was adopted to describe the objectives and criteria for appointment. What is significant here is that the privilege of further study does not depend on academic qualifications alone, but on traits and experiences that Rhodes believed were important in the kind of leader he hoped to encourage.

A more contemporary description of objectives can be seen in the case of the DAAD. While DAAD has had more than a million grantees since 1950 in its two hundred programs, the overarching purpose is summed up in a recent report as:

> . . . encouraging members of the international, young, up-and-coming academic elite to come to Germany for a study or research stay and, as far as possible, of maintaining these contacts as life-long partners, as well as the goal of qualifying young German research scientists at the very best locations around the world in a spirit of tolerance and liberal-minded, cosmopolitan attitudes, of assisting the developing countries of the South as well as the reforming states of the East establish efficient higher education structures and, finally, the goal of maintaining or establishing German studies and the German language, literature and area studies at important universities and colleges around the world at a level worthy of and appropriate to a great cultural nation.[8]

A hundred years apart in terms of public description, they are very similar in spirit and mission. Both sought an appreciation of a cultural tradition by individuals who were considered exceptionally able, even superior. Both saw as a result of exposing superior young people to other systems of education that their own systems of education might be strengthened.

There may be different, sometimes overlapping, missions for the many nationally competitive scholarships, whether these are offered in Europe, Japan, the Commonwealth, the United States, or elsewhere. Among the specified outcomes are:

- Imparting specific substantive skills and knowledge
- Redirecting or raising career objectives
- Strengthening leadership skills
- Encouraging public service
- Increasing international understanding
- Sustaining creativity
- Increasing participation of the underrepresented
- Furthering international mobility
- Developing a global or national perspective or affinity
- Other public goals

For each outcome there are indicators, signs at the point of award that the recipient is likely to achieve what is wanted.

Common to all of them, however, is the need to choose from among the many worthy applicants. For this, in addition to the specific characteristics sought (for example, interest in German culture, biomedical science), those who prevail in these competitions show more "leadership," "talent," and "creativity" than those candidates who do not prevail. Even those programs addressing opportunity for underrepresented groups seek the most "promising" from those considered underrepresented.

Knowing that our candidates are relatively young, it is important to speculate on what they could accomplish by their early or mid-twenties that would convince selection panelists of their superior promise. How does one detect "promise" in individuals so relatively inexperienced? Is it easier to do in the case of field-specific programs such as the Howard Hughes Fellowships in biological science or the Mellon Fellowships in humanities, as opposed to general fellowships such as the Rhodes and Marshall? In contrast, to use an American example, the Guggenheim Fellowship, which is normally given to a scholar or artist in mid-career, those who do the selecting have one or two decades of work to appraise.

What do talent, leadership, and creativity look like when they appear in the credentials of candidates? The chart below seeks to suggest "manifestations" of these three most commonly used criteria. Though used differently, note how similar "talent" and "creativity" are.

TABLE 2: SELECTION MARKERS

Talent	Leadership	Creativity
Public recognition through official results, winning of prizes and other confirmation of quality	Speaks authoritatively for others, as head of publicly recognized group or organization	Expresses self in a complex medium normally associated with older persons
Performance in a medium at a standard normally associated with older individuals	Sustains group to address issue of imputed public importance	Contributes new or different approach to existing formulation

A paper presented by Robert J. Sternberg and Elena L. Grigorenko at the Bellagio conference helped us think about how to be more concrete about what we mean in the selection process by these terms—as well as by "wisdom."[9] In addition, the presence at Bellagio of the former director of the MacArthur Foundation "Genius" awards gave us an opportunity to think about what seems to correlate with the persistence of creativity into mid-career.

Evidence from the Student Development Literature

In addition to the literature reviewed by Sternberg and Grigorenko, it is helpful to look at the literature on student development, with a focus on the conditions that nurture the traits we seek in our finalists. The point of award for many of the scholarship programs represented at Bellagio is at the conclusion of the first university degree. The undergraduate experience, thus, is common to all, and allows us to ask about the nature of undergraduate education and its impact on the most able students. What experiences or environments most encourage those traits we seek? Are there settings in which they are already visible?

The literature is vast on how college affects students and how students can make the most of their college years. Regrettably for an international gathering, only examples from the United States were presented at Bellagio, though all three authors were educated in Britain as well as in the United States. We, however, assume that these characteristics and their relationship to success are found in many systems of higher education.

The student development literature presents its findings across a broad spectrum, from highly quantitative longitudinal studies to the anecdotal and qualitative. On the one hand, some two hundred American colleges and universities and more than twenty thousand students and faculty have participated annually over several decades in a longitudinal study of student attitudes, values, and ambitions.[10] At the other end of the spectrum is a highly qualitative study, drawn from just twenty colleges, of how students can most benefit from college and how faculty can help them.[11] There are literally hundreds of studies that seek to measure how students develop in college.[12]

Social scientists are cautious about establishing cause and effect. A brief summary of the literature, plus a generous sprinkling of common sense derived from nearly half a century in the university, give the authors of this short paper the temerity to suggest some settings, interventions, and events that seem to give students the greatest sense of ambition and confidence.[13]

For those who choose to invest in human capital (and all scholarship programs are such investments), the reassuring answer seems to be "people make the difference." It is particular people and the settings for interaction that create the most powerful influence on the choices and performance of undergraduates—not the size or selectivity of the college, not the major or focus of a curriculum, not visibility or resources of the university, or even how well its faculty is paid.

From all the evidence, it is clear that there are three, sometimes overlapping, undergraduate environments or experiences that have the greatest effect on ambition, confidence, and achievement. They are (1) the stimulation and influence of peers, (2) small group interaction, in and out of class, and (3) the sustained attention of teachers. In support of the strong influence of peers, one large study finds the most significant variable for outcomes in ambition, self-reported learning, and career choice is the peer group of "high intellectual self-esteem."[14] Students generally tend to change their values, behavior, and academic plans in the direction of the dominant orientation of their peer group. From this data, the author asserts that "the values, attitudes, self-concept, and socio-economic status of the peer group are much more important determinants of how the individual student will develop than are the peer group's abilities, religious orientation, or racial composition." Should selection committees be asking a candidate "Who are your friends and what are they doing now?"

Small group interaction is also cited as a powerful teacher. Many faculty and deans assume students respond best when they are respectfully treated as adults, entrusted to do the work and directed to write a long, thoughtful paper at the course's conclusion. For some years we did too. But data supporting learning, intellectual engagement, and passion correlate strongly with courses that are more "interactive." Such courses offer frequent discussion with the professor, require numerous writing assignments often shared with other students, and may demand cooperative homework assignments. The amount of writing is a key indicator. The connection between the amount of writing in a course and a student's engagement in it is dramatic, whether measured by time spent on that course by the intellectual challenge it presented, or just how much the student liked doing the work.[15]

What might be the implication of this finding for selection panels? It is not easy to make a direct connection. Perhaps a key to assessing the quality of the candidate's intellectual experience through the file or an interview could be the amount of writing done in class and how much interaction was possible with the professor. Letters of recommendation may attest to both.

Not far behind the overall effectiveness of the peer group and engaged learning, is, the data suggest, the importance of the positive intervention of a wise advisor. Such a person may, but need not be, associated with an academic class. Some thirty students who had been selected as Rhodes and Marshall Scholars believed that *the* significant factor in their success was that at "key points in their college years, an academic advisor asked questions, or posed a challenge, that forced them to think about the relationship of their academic work to their personal lives."[16] The point here illustrates the importance of an intervention by a respectful adult who engages the student in questions of both making a life and making a living. Such individuals may be especially astute referees. Candidates might be asked to send a recommendation letter from a person he or she considers to be a "mentor" or major professor.

Although certain kinds of institutions, for example liberal arts colleges and prestigious universities, might be more likely to enable settings for small group interaction or attract students who would form peer groups of "high intellectual self-esteem," the findings suggest that such settings and peer group formations occur across many kinds of institutions. They seem to provide the same positive direction for their students. Elite institutions or not, this learning, however, is positively correlated with residential campuses and living away from home.

What specifically does the student development literature say about developing and identifying leadership, that goal that most scholarships say their programs seek? Little research appears useful beyond that fact that election to student office is correlated with strong participation in volunteer, social, literary, artistic enterprises and with intramural sports. Racial and cultural awareness is also "correlated with leadership."[17] Selection panels looking for "demonstrated leadership" need to look beyond the resume and identified campus offices to ad hoc settings to find examples of the initiative, imagination, and judgment so often found in successful leaders.

In sum, there are persuasive data to suggest that in the presence of wise mentors, engaged classes, volunteer leadership, and most particularly a strong intellectual peer group, good things of note can happen to large numbers of undergraduates.

Broadening the Opportunity and Enriching the Experience

All scholarship programs represented at the Bellagio conference indicated that they wanted to draw from broader applicant pools. They aspire to find more grantees outside elite institutions and away from metropolitan cities; they actively seek more racial diversity and a greater socio-economic range. Some scholarships look for greater gender balance.

Over the past three decades what has changed most on American college campuses is the "new student diversity," students bringing their different backgrounds to campus. Many universities have allocated significantly more financial aid to assure this end. Some of the most selective institutions have pushed the hardest to offer access to traditionally barred groups and to assure all students have the experience of learning from a more diverse faculty and student body.

Briefly, what has been the American university experience in pressing for excellence *and* diversity? How, for example, do race aware admissions policies work in practice? In their landmark study, *The Shape of the River*, William Bowen and Derek Bok measured the success of black students admitted to academically selective colleges under race-aware admissions policies to see how well these students met the expectations placed on them.[18] In relation to their white classmates, the study shows that black students functioned well in competitive universities. More particularly, in measures of graduate degrees and entry into the professions, income, life satisfaction, and success in achieving leadership positions in their working and volunteer lives, black students performed very well indeed. Those in the most demanding institutions performed the best of all.

Two other recent studies stress the advantages for all students who attend colleges with such diversity. These studies also emphasize how positively many students regard learning from others with different points of view. Greater self-reported gains in cognitive and affective development and in increased satisfaction in their college experience are positively associated with increased institutional commitment to promoting racial understanding.[19]

What do the data suggest for our efforts to include candidates from new groups in our scholarship awardees? Bowen and Bok suggest that students from diverse backgrounds will use these opportunities no less well than those from the traditional pool, and that the environments for learning will be richer. To conclude, "Clearly, the dire claims about the detrimental effects of emphasizing diversity are not supported by the data. On the contrary, findings suggest that there are many developmental benefits that accrue to students when institutions encourage and support the emphasis on multiculturalism and diversity."[20]

SELECTION

Among the many programs represented at Bellagio, there were dozens of combinations of processes in selection. Some programs allow candidates to nominate themselves; other programs require institutions to pre-select candidates. Some programs are more universalistic in their requirements for candidates, others require distributive (for example, geography, field), often particularistic requirements to be met. Some programs have staff members make final decisions; other programs delegate the decisions to selection panels. Some programs use interviews; others do not. Some programs prepare their interviewers for the responsibility; others assume that formal credentials suffice as preparation. Some programs use their former recipients as selection panelists; others choose panelists because of their public eminence.

To our knowledge, there is little discussion as to which combinations constitute "best practices" in terms of achieving one's mission. If you take the brochures of these programs at face value, you would believe that all these arrangements were determined in light of such discussions. Issues of convenience and eminence, however, affect most arrangements. The amount of attention each application gets depends on its length and the proximity of the application deadline to the interview or final decision schedule; the length of interviews is likely to be determined by the number of candidates to be interviewed, the number of days that interviews can be scheduled, and the length of time panelists can be made available.

Whether to have an interview is a major question. How many? With whom? For how long? In what format? In a personal communication, Allan Goodman, president of the Institute of International Education in the United States, maintained that "there can be a wide variety of nomination, application, and selection processes . . . with no appreciable effect on quality," though he favors "hands-down" nominators plus oral interviews.[21] On the other hand, a reviewer for the National Science Foundation, a program in which interviews are an anathema, argued that actuarial approaches (such as giving numerical status to applicant's department and chief professor, grade point average, scores on the Graduate Record Examination) should be used to check on evaluators and the only value of not using actuarial standards exclusively was that the numbers don't always keep up with changing fields fast enough.[22]

While a strong personal interview can salvage a less meritorious case on paper, interviews are surely a means by which individuals well polished in the presentation of self can secure advantages in competition. Students attending privileged institutions in the United States are often groomed for their interviews by anxious staff. Indeed, the Web site for a very selective American institution offers PowerPoint presentations on how to interview for Rhodes and Marshall scholarships, giving suggestions about clothes, posture, and the way to respond to questions.[23]

NEED FOR PARTNERSHIPS

Selection is never an isolated or even final event. Often other collaborators—partner foundations, governments, and higher educational institutions—need to be enlisted. Not only must the administrators of the Rhodes and Marshall scholarships depend on the recommending colleges and universities to do their work in initial nominations, but they must also secure the agreement of the host colleges and institutions for admissions of their finalists. Fulbright, DAAD, and the Open Society Institute typically depend on cost-sharing with host institutions, other government programs or other foundations. Because of its size and aegis of the European Union, the Erasmus/Socrates program requires very complex departmental agreements to accept work done by students at cooperating institutions, as well as financial calculations on comparative national costs. The new Ford International Fellows Program is even more complex. It relies on non-typical organizations to recommend candidates in the first place and then often chooses as destinations for study institutions without long traditions of educating international students.

In contrast, few nationally competitive scholarship programs have the management autonomy enjoyed by the Thomas J. Watson Foundation or the Paul and Daisy Soros Fellowships for New Americans. While the Watson program depends on selected institutions to make nominations, once the Fellow is appointed the responsibility for the "wanderjahr of one's own devising" rests entirely on the recipient, no sharing with other funders or institutions. The thirty Paul and Daisy Soros Fellows each year are self-nominated and if they fail to gain admissions themselves to graduate programs they forfeit the award. The formal cooperation of no other institution, funder, or government is necessary.

Little has been written on partnerships.[24] What are the conditions for their effective formation, sustaining, and termination? How do new programs earn the "currency of respect" to enlist partners? Are there lead partners? Are partners best enlisted at the outset of programs? What in the Rhodes or Marshall history might help the administrator of the new Gates Cambridge program to manage the complex relationships with Cambridge colleges and graduate programs? What can the administrators of the Commonwealth Fellowships share with the new Ford International Fellows program that would ease recruitment in Africa and Asia and in forming alternatives to expensive advanced degrees in Europe or North America?

ADDED VALUE

Selection is only the beginning. What happens during the course of the scholarship (and after) is a key to whether or not a program's objective will be reached. Readers of biography know the powerful role played by apparent chance in opening doors, enabling projects, or encouraging young aspirants. It would seem worth considering how, as program managers and educators, we can at least influence the circumstances in which constructive chance meetings can or will happen for the recipients of our scholarships.

In the personal communication referred to earlier, Allan Goodman argued that what makes the "difference" is the "enrichment process." He continued: "It is the experience they have while on the scholarship that matters. I suspect the programs which make sure that the winners have a chance to network and support strong alumni programs, promote interaction across generations with established leaders, and convey the impression that a young person should not hesitate to get seized with a set of global issues (beyond their discipline) . . . produce the kinds of persons which we all wish would inherit the earth."[25] Bernd Wächter has expressed a similar sentiment. From his long experience with European Union and other scholarship programs, he believes more time and planning should be spent in the "aftercare" of recipients, in assisting them to become more effective.[26]

Some programs, however, have not shown interest in adding value to their award. They leave this task to the recipients themselves and to the institutions they attend. There is no orientation to the program, no meetings with other holders of the scholarship, no efforts at a newsletter or an association to keep the recipients in touch. The philosophy here, commonly found in corporate assumptions about human capital development, is that true talent, like cream, rises to the top. Able people will create their own opportunities and use them well. Indeed, "making your own way" and learning by mistakes is intrinsic to the philosophy of the Thomas J. Watson Fellowship.

Other programs try, as Allan Goodman advocates, influencing the quality of the scholarship, to make recipients receptive to learning from others as well as becoming thoughtful and self-conscious about their own development. A short cut to powerful learning, as mentioned in the discussion of campus life, could well be the "peer group of high self-esteem." How much these ambitious and differently talented people could teach each other, if only they were brought together to form a group!

Several of the older scholarships have developed highly articulated programs to enrich the scholarship year and provide continuing growth for scholars and connection to the mission of the program. Two programs, the Fulbright and the Rhodes, have goals that aspire to mutual understanding and respect between the scholar and the people of the host country. Both programs hold that a diffusion of talented leaders will make the world a better place. (While Senator Fulbright had a global vision of what such an impact might mean, the Rhodes Scholars were to be a deeply personal cohort motivated to serve their societies—and the alumni programs reflect these differences.) Both programs have invested time and attention to the adjustment of the scholar (and sometimes the family) to the new country, with attention to orientation. Both programs aspire to long-term professional and personal association between scholars and people in the receiving countries.

Specifically, the American Fulbright program typically begins with an orientation for recipients and follows up with in-country conferences for assessment and evaluation. Forty-two countries have Fulbright alumni associations—including Uzbekistan and Burkina Faso. Presumably, these associations do what good alumni do everywhere: sustain relationships and loyalty to the institution, encourage "networking" for opportunities and effectiveness, and build support—financial, political, and intellectual—for the Fulbright program. Out of roughly one hundred thousand American Fulbright recipients, six thousand belong to a Fulbright Alumni Association, which publishes a newsletter and features an annual awards dinner. The association, with alumni in every congressional district, is an important advocate for sustained public funding.

The Rhodes scholarship provides an example of what careful nurture at Oxford and established connection throughout life might look like. Cecil Rhodes did not specify in his will more care than admission to an Oxford college. His successor trustees, however, decided to increase the likelihood of positive outcomes by having a resident counselor, later called the warden of Rhodes House, to be present during the academic term. Although twenty-nine Rhodes scholarships are won each year by nationals from eighteen countries, the American Rhodes organization provides an example of how imaginative "aftercare" might be instituted. Since 1919, there has been an American secretary, paid out of alumni dues. The American secretary organizes the selection process and oversees the publication of a journal, *The American Oxonian,* and a newsletter. Rhodes alumni are active in regional and state selection panels. Alumni regularly organize class reunions in the United States. There have been two national reunions and the Rhodes women have recently met as a group. In its centenary year, the Rhodes Trust hosted international celebrations in both the United

Kingdom and in South Africa. So exercised are some folks about all the efforts of Rhodes scholars to advance each other's interests and to rule the world, that Web sites have popped up to warn the rest of us about Rhodes "aftercare."[27]

In a conference session designed to discuss what kinds of "value added" projects might enhance our programs, we might look at the range of reliable vehicles used by well-run university alumni programs. Some independent American universities and colleges have developed these programs to a high art form and similar approaches are increasingly found in other countries and nonprofit institutions. This range of programs, however, usually has a single purpose: to assure support to the university—through the time, talent, and treasure of its alumni and friends. While our program goals for enriching the scholarship years and for "aftercare" of alumni may differ from those of the university, it is useful to identify the most commonly used programs to achieve these ends.

Among them are:

- Receptions and dinners
- Reunions—with high emotional and intellectual content
- Life-long learning through classes, book groups, faculty-on-the-road, sometimes known as "Road Scholar," etc.
- Educational travel with faculty guides to distant sites
- Service projects, alumni mentoring, internships[28]
- Fundraising for "alumni scholarships," or any university need, through cultural, social, or athletic events
- Magazines, newsletters, class letters
- Admissions recruitment and interviewing
- Advisory and visiting committees to schools, departments, and libraries

Listed above is a formidable array of ways universities engage their alumni. Such approaches occasionally are, and might well increasingly be, employed to engage the loyalty and attention of scholarship recipients and alumni in our programs. Our discussion, then, might focus on how to promote three sets of goals: (1) how to enrich the scholarship year or years; (2) how to increase the likelihood of meeting the scholarship's mission through the lifetime achievement of its scholarship holders; and (3) how to draw on the talents and time of alumni to create a more visible, more effective, and inclusive scholarship.

This conversation might be shaped by the following questions:

- Which of our programs support a set of collateral experiences during the scholarship that most advance the objectives of the program? How do the ongoing activities reinforce the objectives of the program in the form of "orientation," "mentors," and other planned encounters?
- How can the "cohort effect" be harnessed to emphasize and consolidate the ends for which the program exists? Who has specific experience to share of the advantages of creating and using peer groups of common assumptions and "high self-esteem"?
- Do any of us believe that we have post-grant activity that particularly furthers the purposes of our program? Given the many allegiances our recipients have, how much "value added" would have value for the recipient throughout life? Is there any long-term capital the program can draw on, based on the testimonies about the "transforming" experience of the scholarship?
- Finally, what programs of "aftercare" empower the new alumna or alumnus to pursue the achievements, alone and together, for which the scholarship was created in the first place?

EVALUATION

Evaluation is one of the reasons we gathered in Bellagio. How do we evaluate our programs in light of the practices of other programs and effect some improvement? What do other programs do as a practice that affects their results positively? That use of the word evaluation, however, is only part of the larger industry of "evaluation," the formal examination of the practices and results, with a view often of whether to continue to fund such activities. While Cecil Rhodes may not be waiting in eternity to see if the objectives of his will have been achieved in practice, other more contemporary programs have such interests. As a generalization, the more a nationally selective scholarship program depends on government money, the more frequently it is evaluated.[29] A recent evaluation of the mammoth Erasmus/Socrates program of the European Union found that participants liked their mobility experience at another European country's campus, that the experience had not significantly delayed the receiving of a degree, and it had not made an appreciable difference in employment or income, except for those who were engaged in language translation.[30]

A recent evaluation of the American Fulbright program stressed the importance of "the multiplier effects" in achieving the program's goal of increasing mutual understanding, those activities during and after the Fulbright year that communicated American and host country interests to audiences larger than the immediate institution. The evaluation concluded in language perfect for advocating the program to its funders: "Without exception, the Scholars reported that they found their Fulbright experiences to be valuable and that they are proud to have been Fulbright Scholars. Ninety-seven percent agreed that they would like to obtain another Fulbright grant. This level of approbation is extremely rare in program evaluation research."[31]

There is no good history of evaluations of privately supported competitive scholarship programs. Though it has been much the subject of analysis, the Rhodes program has not—to our knowledge—been subject to an evaluation of its methods and outcomes. After thirty years of supporting graduate education in the basic sciences for medical school faculty, the Markle Foundation could announce that it had assisted education of faculty at every medical school in the United States and then conclude its program.[32] Quite favorable evaluations for the Danforth-Kent Fellows program and the Woodrow Wilson Fellows program were completed shortly before they lost their funding from private foundations.[33] The Thomas J. Watson Foundation has faithfully evaluated its program every decade or so and has made programmatic changes on the basis of their recommendations. Martha Loerke, program director for the Open Society Institute Scholarship programs and Bernd Wächter, who evaluated her program, both participated in the discussion at Bellagio.

An optimistic sign regarding evaluation is that the Ford Foundation International Fellows program has built this process in at the beginning. In addition to several independent studies about the program, "the Center for Higher Education Policy Studies (CHEPS) at the University of Twente in the Netherlands will design an evaluation framework for IFP that will be applied as of 2004, in order to incorporate the results—to the extent possible—while the program is still in progress. The evaluation will assess the program's decentralized design, implementation, and educational effects, including the Fellows' academic placements and performance, completion rates and subsequent employment. Particular emphasis will be given to the recruitment and selection processes to thirteen international sites and whether they are reaching the program's target groups. The quality of placement and monitoring services and the impact of leadership training and cohort-building activities will also be evaluated."[34]

In a paper for the Bellagio conference, Michele Lamont brought her own experience in evaluating scholarship programs to dissect the various stages in the decision process—from building the applicant pool to completion of the grant—to show where processes may affect outcomes. On the larger question of how well the various programs have chosen recipients relative to their goals, she rightly pointed out that "success" is situational and affected by factors outside the control of the program.[35] Moreover, we know little about the life trajectories of those not selected. And then there is the double-blind question of evaluation: how did others not associated with the program appear to achieve those same goals?

There is also the ultimate question of evaluation: the opportunity cost of the nationally competitive scholarship programs. This has seldom been considered. Andrew Carnegie built libraries; he did not give fellowships. Are the roads to the ends of the donors better served by competitive scholarships than other possibilities? We believe so, but it is surely worth the discussion.

Conclusions

We believe awarding scholarships to young people is a profoundly moral activity. To advance promising youth on their careers and at the same time advance the values of our donors and societies is a rare opportunity. We believe that the pool of applicants should be coterminous with all the aspiring and able young people capable of undertaking the work and pursuing the ends to which the scholarship is dedicated. We believe that determining the values in selection should be as concretely specified as possible and that the process by which finalists are determined be as robust, uniform and insightful as it can be. We believe that what happens during and after the scholarship tenure should receive the same kind of attention and imagination as is invested in the selection process. Finally, we look to a form of evaluation that is timely and useful, and that does not merely justify our programs' futures. In all of this, we go forward in modesty, bearing in mind the words of a contemporary, borrowing from the ancient Greeks: "Whom the gods wish to destroy they first call promising."

11

Keys To The United Kingdom

ELIZABETH VARDAMAN

Elizabeth Vardaman, associate dean in the College of Arts and Sciences and associate director of the honors program at Baylor University, Waco, Texas, has taught at Baylor since 1980. An exchange professor in China and assistant director for several Baylor abroad programs in England and the Netherlands, she has traveled extensively on behalf of the university and led the first NAFA tour of British higher education. She has been serving as a scholarship advisor since 1998 and was a charter member of the National Association of Fellowship Advisors. "NAFA in the United Kingdom— Review and Preview" was a panel discussion offered at the 2003 national

NAFA conference by participants from the inaugural NAFA trip to England and Scotland, which took place May 25–June 7, 2002. Panelists included Mark Bauer (Yale University), Carrie Devine (University of California-Davis), Paula Goldsmid (Pomona College), Jane Morris (Villanova University), and Vardaman, the 2002 trip coordinator.[1]

The NAFA tour 2002 provided thirty-two NAFA members[2] a memorable overview of graduate programs at many British institutions of higher education and gave us an opportunity to understand better how we may serve our students who wish to study at these prestigious schools.

The trip began in London with conversations with the British Council, followed by discussions with university administrators and tours of the University of Westminster, The School of Oriental and African Studies, Imperial College, and the London School of Economics. We then proceeded to Oxford and Cambridge, where we met with the heads of the prestigious scholarship trusts, including the warden of Rhodes House and the provost of the Gates Cambridge Trust, as well as visited both the renowned "Ox-bridge" colleges and the "new" Oxford Brookes. The trip then headed to the north of England, where we met with officials at York University and Durham, then to Scotland for meetings at the University of Edinburgh and University of St. Andrews. Meetings in Scotland included a reception with representatives from a number of other Scottish universities and with the British Council Scotland.

What did we learn that will enable us to guide our students more effectively as they conduct research and try to discriminate among the impressive array of British universities? Below are some of the insights, resources, and electronic materials that were presented by the panel; also included are highlights from the meetings and discussions that took place during and following the 2002 tour.

Understanding the General Structure of Postgraduate Education

Throughout our visit to England and Scotland, university officials affirmed that a recent shift had taken place; prestigious scholarship applications are now less frequently directed toward second bachelor of arts degree and more often toward graduate programs. Unless students have a compelling reason to broaden or change their major field of study, many British academics view the taught master's degree a better use of the student's energies and focus.[3] The increase in numbers of taught master's degrees is encouraging news for many NAFA members, who see this option as providing a much less stressful transition into graduate study than the direct step into a research degree from the American undergraduate structure. For these and other reasons, this report emphasizes the graduate school experience, resources, and structures (although some undergraduate resources are also included).

Within the graduate education conversation, one of the first issues advisors and students must consider is the distinction made between "research programs" (which are offered at both the master's and doctorate level) and "taught courses of study" (which are offered only at the master's degree level). For example, students may choose a one-year master of arts degree in either a research or taught program at Durham University, but an MPhil there could possibly take two years to complete, depending on the program. Some MPhil degrees at Durham contain both taught components and a thesis; others rely solely on research. Confused? It is easy to be.

Mark Bauer has compiled a list of the degrees offered by the universities visited on the NAFA 2002 trip (see Appendix A). No matter which degree titles a university uses, however, students will want to understand the following distinctions as they begin their search for the "course" that best fits their goals:

- Some master's degrees are built largely on taught courses of study, culminating usually in a ten thousand to twenty thousand word thesis (the British would say "dissertation"). These courses may last one or two years.
- The research master's degree can be a one- or two-year course. A master's by research culminates in a research paper of approximately forty thousand words.
- Doctoral degrees (PhD or DPhil) will take three years minimum to complete and require much more research that culminates in the dissertation.

Electronic and Media Sources for Finding the Right Course of Study

With more than one hundred universities in the United Kingdom, a complex nomenclature for degrees, some hard-to-understand vocabulary (even if we speak the same language),[4] and a structure for undergraduate and graduate programs that differs significantly from the American system, students—even our most outstanding ones—face many challenges as they attempt to make sense of their options and find a good match between their academic interests and the courses of study offered within the English and Scottish universities. However, the resources available for the search are impressive, and the British Council's education and training advisor Robert Monro provided NAFA members an overview of the extensive assessment systems they and their students may use.[5]

Two Ratings Systems for Taught Courses of Study (Undergraduate and Graduate)

THE TEACHING QUALITY ASSESSMENT (TQA) RATING SYSTEM

"A part of the audit [mandated by the Quality Assurance Agency] is a subject review called the Teaching Quality Assessment (TQA). A panel of faculty from other institutions is appointed by the QAA to conduct the review. As of 2001 all courses in all subjects had been reviewed. The results are helpful in evaluating the suitability of a taught course for a particular student, though those seeking research degrees would find the RAE more helpful."[6]

LEAGUE TABLES: THEIR VALUE AND LIMITATION

"University League Tables are published by several newspapers in the UK, and function rather like the *US News and World Report* rankings in the US. Some of the tables are self-fulfilling and others show signs of circularity. They undeniably add value to highly rated institutions, however.

- *The Times Good University Guide*:
  http://www.timesonline.co.uk/section/0,,716,00.html
- The *Guardian*: http://www.EducationGuardian.co.uk/
  universityguide[7]

Predictably the tables are controversial; they can be useful if applied thoughtfully.

Strengths / Limitations of the Research Assessment Exercise (RAE) Graduate Study Only

A VALUABLE TOOL

The Research Assessment Exercise is conducted "by peer faculty on behalf of the funding councils. It occurs every five years, most recently in 2001. Quality in every subject area is independently assessed on a seven-point scale: 1, 2, 3b, 3a, 4, 5, and 5* (the highest).[8] Ratings determine funding allocations. . . . A 5* rating identifies a program more than half of whose staff are world-class and the rest nationally known; a 4 has all of the staff with at least a national reputation. . . . The RAE results can be accessed at http://www.hero.ac.uk/rae/."[9]

TWO CAUTIONARY TALES

Paula Goldsmid offers this advice on the Pomona Web site: "Most important: If you aspire to a research degree you must connect with someone who wants to supervise your project. Do not assume that all 5* departments will include your specialty or offer a degree for which you are qualified, so use the RAE as a first step and proceed from there to detailed information on university websites."

Mark Bauer concurs, reminding us that "RAE results are at least three years old and are at once too general and too focused on an assessment of faculty research to represent 'the last word' on any specific degree program or course of study. . . . Thus, the faculty in a 5* history department may do splendid research in many historical fields, but not in the specific area that fits a student's interests. Similarly, key faculty in a 5* department may not be teaching or available to supervise research."

Search Tools for Taught and Research Postgraduate Courses

The Prospects site at http://www.prospects.ac.uk offers a search of 17,550 postgraduate programs within the United Kingdom. Students should go

to "Further Study" to begin. Robert Monro alerted us to the multifunc-
tional searches, saying "The web-site can be searched by institution, by
subject, or by key words. This allows you either to select where you would
like to study and then see what they offer; or to select what you would like
to study and see where it is available; or to search the database using a few
key words to see what combination of locations and subjects are available."[10] The keyword search is very useful and does not limit one to names
of major subjects. The site offers this example: "[A] search for courses in
the subject area Town and Country Planning at all institutions returns 121
courses, whereas a keyword search on Urban Regeneration returns 14
courses."

UNDERGRADUATE AND GRADUATE
ASSISTANCE FROM THE BRITISH COUNCIL

Robert Monro also directed us "to the newly redesigned British Council
web site: http://www.educationuk.org, which is a great resource for students seeking to find the right course [of study]. They can enter key
words, the type of course, the location of the university, etc., and generate
a list of possibilities (randomly ordered). Clicking on an entry lets you
view the details, with links to the TQA and the RAE rankings. . . . The
same procedure can be followed for undergraduate or post-graduate programs." [11]

The British Council USA Web site is also valuable and is being updated
frequently, it can be found at http://www.britishcouncil-usa.org/learn-
ing/index.shtml. This Web site offers the same database as the United
Kingdom version but with additional helpful information for American
students, including an in-depth database of scholarships (described later in
this document). The following link goes directly to the university search
function: http://www.britishcouncil-usa.org/learning/eduk/index.html.
The British Council USA has also developed a Web site for advisors and
offers handbooks and comprehensive guidebooks at this location: http://
www.britishcouncilusa.org/learning/advisors/advisor_resources.shtml.

In December of 2001, Robert Monro sent a document to NAFA enti-
tled "Finding the Right Postgraduate Course of Study in the UK." It out-
lines a suggested series of steps to help students find the course of study
that fits their field and enables them to review evaluations of those courses
of study. (See Appendix C.)

Building a Network of Personal Contacts

Keeping the difficult balance between quantitative and qualitative sources is a clear message NAFA members heard during the trip. Mark Bauer spoke well to the need for such balance in a recent conversation we had via e-mail, "Research [into the rankings and assessment tools] not only helps make better matches but also makes the students stronger because they become more knowledgeable and self-aware candidates for funding. Nevertheless, Master's programs can be of uneven quality at any university, and college choice (for students applying to graduate or second BA programs at Cambridge or Oxford) adds another element of uncertainty. For these reasons, it is very important for students to use their networks to discover as much about the programs (and colleges) they are considering as possible." Here then are a few reminders to balance against ratings.

ENCOURAGE STUDENTS TO CONTACT THE FACULTY

Monro gives a hint in the handout referenced above that bears repeating here: "Having looked at all these sites you will probably have found one or more courses that will suit you. If you want more information about any of these, do not be afraid to e-mail or telephone the [faculty] member responsible for them, with specific questions you want answered. Most academics are only too happy to talk to prospective students about their courses and encourage them to join!"

Gordon Johnson, president of Wolfson College, Cambridge and provost of the Gates Cambridge, would support that recommendation: "It is definitely advisable for the student to make preliminary contact with a potential PhD advisor." [12] For master's degrees questions, student inquiries may be directed to admissions@gradstudies.cam.ac.uk. [13]

Mark Bauer adds, "Students should not be shy about making inquiries concerning particular programs, how they are structured, who is teaching or supervising research. . . . But students should beware of pestering with questions that are answered on department or program websites. They should be advised that any inquiry is also something of an audition, in that it will leave an impression (and an e-mail or paper record) about how suitable the student seems."

Throughout the trip, administrators and faculty members offered us their cards and encouraged us to contact them or have our students do so.

For example, at Oxford we were told Jan Power (jan.power@admin.ox. ac.uk) can offer guidance on graduate programs—however, students "are urged to do their homework on the web" as well. We knew these programs had smart, professional people behind them; feeling free to contact individuals at British Council or any of the universities following the trip was one of the deeply appreciated outcomes.

REMIND STUDENTS THAT THEIR OWN PROFESSORS WILL HAVE CONTACTS AND SUGGESTIONS

Paula Goldsmid has valuable information to this effect posted on the Pomona Web site: "Ask faculty in your field of interest what they know about leading departments and scholars in their subject in Britain, and whether anyone in their professional network can help you in your exploration of degree courses." Students should also make contact with British visiting scholars or guest speakers who might suggest other networking possibilities.

ENCOURAGE STUDENTS TO BE CREATIVE IN THE SEARCH TO FIND SCHOLARS UNDER WHOM THEY WISH TO STUDY

"If you are applying for a research degree program, do a literature search on your topic to find the specialists in Britain. Use the internet to see what their research centers, labs, and departments are doing currently. Contact the scholar directly, describing your background and your proposed project for graduate research, to inquire about the possibility of working under his or her supervision."[14]

HELP STUDENTS DEVELOP NETWORKS WITH OTHER STUDENTS

In an end-of-the-trip visit among NAFA members, one advisor who had visited with former students at various universities throughout our travels commented that students often didn't realize how different study in the United Kingdom would turn out to be, compared to their United States experiences or expectations. Thus, it is "extremely helpful for students to be able to talk with other students either currently enrolled or recently graduated from the programs they are considering. These students often have important tips for those who follow them. Often these contacts are made circuitously: referrals through friends of friends."

Other "Ah-ha's!"

The NAFA travelers met twice during the second week to reflect on the issues that had been most clearly etched in our minds. Some of the issues that seem most important to our understanding the United Kingdom system of graduate education and resources are listed below:

UNDERSTANDING THE "OLD" AND THE "NEW" UNIVERSITIES

"Of the 100 or so [British] universities, all have an identical general mission. Small, legal structural differences distinguish two categories: the 'old' (pre-1992) and the 'new' (post 1992) universities. The Old Universities are universally research universities ranging in age from 40–800 years old. . . . In contrast the New Universities tend to be urban and large; they emphasize teaching but have pockets of research excellence. They were formed from former polytechnic institutes, and in 1992 were granted status as corporations by the higher education act of Parliament." [15]

THE EVER-CLOSER RELATIONSHIP AMONG FOUNDATIONS

In inspiring meetings with John Rowett, warden of Rhodes House, and Gordon Johnson, provost of the Gates Cambridge Trust, we understood clearly that the foundations were striving to work together, not viewing themselves as competitors, but rather as united in their commitment to academics, service, and leadership. Rowett reminded us there are plenty of top scholar-applicants from whom the Fulbright, Kennedy, Gates, Marshall, Rhodes, and other foundations may choose.

THE WISDOM OF LOOKING BEYOND LONDON, OXFORD, AND CAMBRIDGE FOR THE RIGHT COURSE FOR THE MARSHALL APPLICANT

"Students *must* have thought about their selection of program and university. Many elect Oxford, and indeed many go there, but each year Oxford rejects several, usually because they have selected competitive courses such as International Relations, which are already full. In such cases placement is offered in the second-choice school. It is a distinct advantage to have found good reasons to study at schools other than the Big Three. To identify appropriate courses, use the web. Contact academics at the university; use e-mail to contact potential departments. . . . The Marshall website has many useful links: http://www.marshallscholarship.org/links.html and so does the graduate career website: www.prospects.ac.uk."[16]

THE DIFFERENCES IN THE ENGLISH AND THE
SCOTTISH SYSTEMS OF HIGHER EDUCATION

The English system (which includes Wales and Northern Ireland) is a highly specialized undergraduate program that is typically three years in duration. The Scottish-based undergraduate education (which they describe as a combination of tradition and innovation) is a four-year program and culminates in an undergraduate thesis. The Scottish system is structured more like the American system, with students taking a general education the first two years and beginning their specialization in the third year. Another major difference between "ancient universities" of Scotland and the "old" institutions of England is that there is no collegiate system in Scottish schools.

THE RAE RANKING SYSTEM MAY BE IMPERFECT—NEVERTHELESS

Universities find meaning in their scores and refer to their excellent ratings with understandable pride. The following items are *not* comprehensive overviews of programs, but are highlights from notes. I present nine of the eleven universities we visited, omitting only Oxford and Cambridge universities because of their well-known, numerous strengths. These are listed only to make the point that RAE ratings have significant resonance in presentations of United Kingdom universities. For example,

- The University of Westminster in London (a "new university") told us it had earned "5s" in law, Asian studies, and linguistics.
- London School of Economics stated proudly that it had earned 5* in accounting, anthropology, economics, finance, international history, law, and philosophy—among others.
- The department of anthropology and sociology at the School of Oriental and African Studies received a 5 in the 2001 RAE.
- Imperial College says it is the premier technological institution in the world, with every research group a 5* (that is to say, internationally recognized).
- Oxford Brookes (also a "new university") takes special pride in its history department's research 5* rating, noting that Oxford University had only a 5 in the same category.[17]

- The University of York excels in English studies and psychology at 5* level and describes its computer science department as "top in the UK."
- Six divisions of University of Durham received 5* (applied math, chemistry, English, geography, history and law).
- St. Andrews in Scotland presents proudly its international security degree (with terrorism specialty and Al Qaeda studies), its English and psychology programs, saying that all departments at the university were at least 4s, many were 5 and 5*.
- The University of Edinburgh states on its graduate Web site, "During the most recent UK Research Assessment Exercise, the University of Edinburgh maintained its position as one of the foremost research universities in the United Kingdom." The university is described by many as rivaling Cambridge in the biological sciences.

FINDING HELP THROUGH THE UNITED KINGDOM COUNCIL FOR OVERSEAS STUDENT AFFAIRS

"[This] office [recently renamed The Council for International Education] provides assistance with immigration and other regulatory issues, guidance and sign posts for students to measure their progress, and advice line for students and staff. [This] website, www.ukcosa.org.uk includes 28 titles of useful manuals to guide students."[18]

LOCATING FUNDING BEYOND THE NATIONALLY COMPETITIVE AWARDS

The British Council USA Web site offers a scholarship database listing over 125 scholarships and includes detailed resources for using American federal financial aid as well, at http://www.britishcouncil-usa.org/learning/students/fundingscholarships/index.shtml. One scholarship in particular was referenced on several occasions during the NAFA visit: "The Overseas Research Scholarship supports 1,000 international students per year, paying the difference between the domestic and overseas tuition charge (about 6,000 pounds sterling) for up to three years. You can use this award to extend a one-year Fulbright, for example."[19] One NAFA member explains the importance of this information: "I learned that there are other scholarships for overseas students. . . . Actually, after one of my Gates applicants was turned down I encouraged him to apply to LSE, which he did, and he was accepted. I don't know if he has gotten an ORS yet, but I definitely knew to tell him to apply, which I would not have otherwise."

TWO FINE WEB SITE MODELS THAT PRESENT BRITISH OPTIONS CLEARLY

If you have not looked at Paula Goldsmid's scholarship Web site at http://www.pomona.edu/adwr/fellowships/researchbritish.shtml, you will want to do so very soon. It speaks directly to the students, giving them the best of everything we learned on the trip. Yale's Web site, http://www.yale.edu/iefp/fellowships/index.html, provides a tremendously rich overview of the best materials gleaned from our trip and undoubtedly from other sources as well. Many other schools, of course, have created terrific guideposts on the Web for the enterprising students already. For those who have not yet utilized this resource fully, Pomona and Yale certainly give fine models by which to refurbish Web sites.

Reflections from NAFA Members

The following comments, selected from numerous e-mails and letters received following the tour, are important—not only because they affirm the 2002 trip, but also because they affirm NAFA and the people who comprise our fine national organization.

- "In providing alternate universities in the Marshall app, for example, it is invaluable to know more about 'other' U's in the UK. Even better to visit them and get a real feel. It really is a lot about which U's are best in what fields."
- "I did very much enjoy dinner at Wolfson, Cambridge—exposure to the variety of people who visit & study there—even though we were grubby from the road, it didn't matter. It's on my mind now because our Gates Cambridge finalist who just interviewed wants to go there if she wins one."
- "I wanted to tell you all how much I enjoyed being with you during the past two weeks, but especially the last week when we could get to know each other better. It was a privilege to work with you all, and an absolute pleasure to get to know each of you. So much of

what made this trip memorable and valuable had to do with the ideas, experiences, and, yes, the humor, that you each brought 'to the table,' and I am very grateful."

- "There were many ways that my NAFA sponsored trip benefited our prestigious scholarship program. There was the networking aspect, of being with other scholarship advisors 24/7, the sharing of ideas and experiences. There was the insight, like talking personally to the Warden of the Rhodes Trust about one of our current applicants. There were the contacts. I received business cards of individuals from each institution that my students could then contact directly to have their questions answered. There was the alternative prospectus from Cambridge. There was the information we learned about the rating system from the British Council, I doubt I would have been able to learn as much on my own from reading alone."

- "Five years ago when we created our office, our university had won two nationally competitive awards in the previous year: one Fulbright and one NSEP. Affiliation with NAFA, including and especially the trip to the UK, has enabled us to develop and build a strong program to where last year our students won fourteen awards, and this year two of our students won Marshall Scholarships—the first ever at our campus. There are many reasons for this success, but key among them are the information and ideas gleaned during conferences, meetings and trips, and, even more importantly, the relationships with valued and trusted colleagues developed and sustained through those activities."

- "In terms of helping with our students specifically, it is no coincidence I am sure that our campus had its first Marshall scholar since 1974 (and the 3rd in our history) 3 months after I returned from England."

- "For all that has been—Thanks! To all that shall be—Yes!"[20]

I am particularly indebted to David Chaundler, Bursar of Westminster School in London, for the magical evening tour he gave us of Westminster Abbey. John Harris of Christ Church, Oxford, spared no efforts or expense in welcoming us for evensong, a tour of the college (complete with tea), and dinner—an evening that captured for us the exhilaration of what it must feel like to be Harry Potter, or perhaps, since we also care about reality, what it must feel like for our scholar-students to walk the halls where the student William Gladstone, prime minister four times, had also walked, 150 years before.

The ideals of the Rhodes Scholarship and the new Mandela-Rhodes initiative, as presented to us at Rhodes House by its warden John Rowett, lifted our spirits and forged our resolve to send forth our best candidates, those who may be the future leaders in a needy world. And we give heartfelt appreciation again to the extra effort Gordon Johnson has invested in NAFA and in helping us understand the Gates Cambridge "scheme." The evening provided at Wolfson College, Cambridge, will always be an unforgettable one, a touchstone of all we dream the academic life should be.

And for those of us who extended our trip to the North of England and Scotland, we will always owe Ann Brown a debt of thanks for creating a farewell party to end all farewell parties at Prestonfield House in Edinburgh.

Almost every one—guide, bus driver, academics, professional staff within the United Kingdom's system—gave us a glimpse into British culture and education that enabled us to turn toward home with better understandings than we had brought with us. We returned to the United States a bit heavier, too—not just from scones and cream but also from the Cambridge lecture lists, the prospectuses from many universities, the business cards, and the books we carried. Perhaps those we met learned something from us, too. Most of us sensed that many university officials had had no idea what fellowship advisors were or what our work might be. Now they do.

Thanks to the wonderful planning team (Ann Brown, Suzanne McCray, and Mary Tolar), to Babs Baugh (friend and travel agent), and to all the NAFA fellow travelers. The weeks had many challenges in the planning and in the operational stages. Everyone was gracious about the high points and the low. I have to hope we all felt, at the end of the day, that the game had been worth the candle. Special thanks to my husband, James, the British historian who gave me the courage to see the project through.

The universities left an indelible impression on us. We saw firsthand that the house of learning in the United Kingdom is a serious one. The commitment to quality education remains central to all academic enterprises, despite great concerns about funding. Without question, our best and brightest students deserve every chance we can give them to study there.

Appendix A: Nomenclature and Degrees

A glance at the chart below will show that there is little rhyme or reason to British degree nomenclature. What I have found most helpful is to tell students that the terminology varies from institution to institution and that they should not to be overly concerned about the names (just follow the terminology provided by the university prospectus). The important distinction they need to consider is between a taught degree and a research degree. I tell them that taught master's programs will usually have a thesis component as well as or in place of an exam, but that the research for these degrees grows out of their coursework and is usually limited to a forty-thousand- to sixty-thousand-word dissertation. Students do not need to have a thesis topic established coming into a taught program, whereas for a research degree they should have a very clear idea of their topic. Students may also want to determine whether a particular taught degree (diploma or master's) might count toward a research degree (master's or doctorate), and they need to be sure of the duration of the particular degree program: nine month, twelve month, one year, or three year.

FIRST DEGREES:

Degree	Duration	Location
BA	3 year	England
MA	4 year	Scotland

POSTGRADUATE DEGREES:

Degree	Duration	Location	
Diplomas/Certificates	9 months (usually)	(Usually taught component of master's w/o dissertation)	

MASTERS DEGREES:

Taught Masters:

Degree	Duration	Location
MA	I year	Durham, LSE (in area studies), SOAS, Westminster (often in arts subjects)
MPhil	I year (usually)	Cambridge (may count toward requirements for PhD, MSc, or Mlitt) LSE (taught component of PhD)
MPhil	2 year	Oxford (largely in arts/humanities subjects)
BPhil	2 year	Oxford (only in philosophy, equivalent to MPhil in other subjects)
MSc	I year	Oxford (by coursework in largely science subjects), LSE (9–12 months), SOAS, Durham, Westminster, Imperial

MBA	Business
LLM	Law
MTh	Theology
MFA	Fine Arts
Mmu	Music

Research Masters:

Degree	Duration	Location
MA	1 year	Durham
MPhil	1–2 year	Durham (years depends on department)
MPhil	2 year	LSE, SOAS, Westminster (may be first two years of PhD), Imperial
MPhil	1 year	Cambridge (in sciences and medicine)
MSc	2 year	Cambridge
MSc	1 year (min.)	Oxford (research in sciences)
MSc	1 year	Durham
MLitt	2 year	Cambridge
MLitt	2 year	Oxford (research in arts and social studies subjects)
MRes	1 year	York (in science and technology subjects), Imperial (in certain courses)

Doctorate Degrees:

PhD	3 year (min.)	Cambridge, Durham, LSE, SOAS, Westminster, Imperial
DPhil	3 year (min.)	Oxford

(Compiled by Mark Bauer, Yale University)

Appendix B: Glossary of British Education Terms

These definitions were compiled from some Web sites, the Ledbetter diary, and conversations held among NAFA travelers. Stephen Prickett, director of the Armstrong-Browning Library at Baylor and a citizen of Britain, spoke with me regarding several of these terms, cautioning me that there are no hard and fast rules with usage of many of these words.

College means a residential unit within the university where students live, eat, and socialize. In some university structures, the college shares teaching responsibilities with the larger university. In others (such as Cambridge and Oxford), the college is responsible for undergraduate education in its entirety from admission through graduation, including formal instruction and student life activities. In Scotland, however, the word *college* most often refers only to the building, as in "New College" at University of Edinburgh, which signifies a particular building.

Course means "course of study"—that is, a whole program of study leading to a degree or a diploma. We might use the term "major area" interchangeably with it.

Diploma is often used to signify a postgraduate taught program that does not include a thesis (or the British would say, a dissertation). It is also used to describe a course of study that covers a practical rather than an intellectual skill—cookery, car maintenance, or photography. For example, someone might take a post-graduate diploma in education (a practical course mostly of classroom skills), whereas a *degree* in education is usually three years and has a stronger intellectual component.

Dissertation and *thesis* are loosely overlapping terms that may in some settings be used interchangeably. However, generally, a dissertation is shorter than a thesis, which is usually expected to contain some original or research component. A one-term course might well be followed by a dissertation (a paper usually of five thousand to twenty thousand words); a PhD is always examined by thesis.

Faculty is a department or a larger unit of administration.

League tables are the media rankings (such as our *U.S. News and World Report* rankings).

A *module* is a unit of instruction. We would use the word *course* in the United States.

A *scheme* is a strategic plan, such as, "There is a host scheme for housing international students." It is most often used to describe a funding source, such as "are you here on a Gates, ORS, or another scheme?"

Staff are the academic professors—as in the statement "Seventy-five percent of the staff at University of Edinburgh are in 5* research departments."

A *tutor* is a university officer who is responsible for teaching and supervising undergraduates in small groups or privately. Sometimes the term is used for a graduate advisor.

A *unit of assessment* refers to a subject or an area of study. For example, politics and international studies on the RAE is described as: "Comparative, area, national and sub-national politics; public administration and policy studies, including science and technology policy; political behavior and political sociology, including gender; political theory and philosophy, including history of political thought; international relations, including strategic, war and peace studies, international political economy and foreign policy analysis; methods in political studies, and higher education pedagogic research."

Appendix C: Finding the Right Postgraduate Course of Study in the United Kingdom

Most of the information you will need [in order to find the right post-graduate course of study] is publicly available through the World Wide Web and can be accessed through HERO, the new site including the former National Information Services and Systems site at http://www.hero.ac.uk/studying/course_information3106.cfm.

1. Decide on the subject area that interests you and whether you wish to take a taught course or study for a postgraduate qualification by research.
2. Look at the postgraduate prospects databases, giving details of all taught courses and research opportunities at United Kingdom universities: http://www.prospects.csu.ac.uk. This Web site also provides some useful background information for international students wanting to go to the United Kingdom. The Web site can be searched by institution, by subject, or by keywords. This allows you either to select where you would like to study and then see what they offer; or to select what you would like to study and see where it is available; or to search the database using a few key words to see what combination of locations and subjects are available.
4. Each entry on the database provides you with some basic information about the course and the institution you have selected, including costs and how to apply, but there is much more information available.

Every university has its own Web site and a full list of these is available at http://www.hero.ac.uk/universities_and_colleges/listing.cfm. These Web sites are not all the same, but by exploring them intelligently you can usually find a full prospectus for the course you are interested in and information about the institution and the staff who will teach or supervise your course. You should be able to judge from this whether it is the right one for you or not.

You can also get independent assessments of the quality of teaching and research in most subject areas at most universities as follows: The outcomes of independent teaching quality assessments are published by the Quality Assurance Agency for Higher Education (QAA) and are available on http://www.qaa.ac.uk/revreps/subjrev/intro.htm. This is quite a complex site but with some exploration you should be able to find the information you want about the courses you are interested in. If you wish to compare different institutions offering similar courses, look first at the "subject overview reports" (http://www.qaa.ac.uk/revreps/subjrev/overviews.htm). These usually have a summary table near the end of the report that can help identify the "best" institutions. Then look at the full subject reports for individual institutions at http://www.qaa.ac.uk/revreps/subjrev/byinstname.htm.

The Research Assessment Exercise (RAE) is carried out every five years to evaluate the research published by most departments in United Kingdom universities. The results are published by the Higher Education Funding Councils on their Web site at http://www.hero.ac.uk/rae/Results/. Again, this is quite a complex site but with a bit of effort you should be able to find the information you need.

Having looked at all these sites you will probably have found one or more courses that will suit you. If you want more information about any of these do not be afraid to e-mail or telephone the staff member responsible for them, with specific questions you want answered. Most academics are only too happy to talk to prospective students about their courses and encourage them to join!

Two things that may be of concern to you, and to the providers of postgraduate courses in the United Kingdom, are your level of English, if you are not a native speaker, and your existing qualifications.

If your understanding and use of English is not up to the appropriate level, you will have great difficulty in following your course, discussing topics with your tutors, and writing a dissertation or thesis for examination at the end of it. You may therefore have to withdraw from the course, or you may fail to get your qualification, both of which benefit no one. You are therefore likely to be asked to demonstrate your competence in English before you are accepted onto a course. This is usually done by taking an IELTS (International English Language Testing Scheme) test, which can be arranged by most British Council offices.

If you are uncertain about whether your existing qualifications will be accepted for entry onto a particular course, you should discuss this with the course leader. They or the university's international office should be able to establish the "equivalence" of your qualifications in the United Kingdom and decide whether they are adequate for entry to the course. If you would like to establish the equivalence of your qualifications for yourself, you can do this through the National Academic Recognition Information Centre (NARIC). Details of their services are available on http://www.naric.org.uk.

(Source: Robert Monro, Higher Education Advisor, British Council, December 2001)

12

Surveying the Profession

A Guide To National Scholarship Advising

JAMES DUBAN, MARY ENGEL, AND RICHARD BADENHAUSEN

James Duban is professor of English and director of the Office for Nationally Competitive Scholarships at the University of North Texas. He has published books and articles in the field of American literature and is a founding board member of the National Association of Fellowships Advisors. He created University of North Texas's Office for Nationally Competitive Scholarships in 1993 and has directed it since that time.

Mary Engel serves as the university director of fellowship programs and the director of medical school placement at The University of Scranton. Prior

to her appointment as fellowships programs director in 2000, she served
The University of Scranton for fourteen years as the associate dean of the
College of Arts and Sciences, the director of the Arts and Sciences advising
center, and director of study abroad. She is also an associate professor of
English.

Richard Badenhausen, professor of English and the Kim T. Adamson
chair, is the director of the Westminster College honors program in Salt Lake
City, Utah. He offers honors courses on a variety of topics including
Shakespeare, film and fiction, the literature of World War I. He coordinates
the scholarship effort at Westminster College. He is publishing a book, T. S.
Eliot and the Art of Collaboration, *with Cambridge University Press in*
2005.

The NAFA survey report consists of questions that surfaced between 2001 and 2003. Some of the questions emerged from the 2001 NAFA conference in Tulsa, Oklahoma, where a seven-person committee inquired into institutional support for the national scholarship endeavor. Break-out sessions allowed conference-goers to discuss their administrative needs and the levels of support at their universities. Most of the people who led breakout sessions sent their notes to Mary Engel (The University of Scranton), who collated and posted those responses in an e-mail document sent to all NAFA members. So the summary was truly a panoramic shot of NAFA members' concerns. In 2003, we drew upon several of those concerns to help create the online survey below.

Richard Badenhausen (Westminster College) and Jim Duban (University of North Texas) added other questions. We then solicited NAFA board input and, on the basis of helpful responses, refined the survey's questions and emphases to make them applicable to as many advising scenarios as possible.

We had a superb response rate to the survey, in large part because University of North Texas's Rich Harrington posted the questions online and constructed an instrument that offered NAFA members immediate access to statistics reflecting responses to each question. We thereby provided every NAFA member with immediate knowledge of the relative level of support of his or her institution. The aim here was to convey enough hard data to allow members to approach their supervisors with compelling facts in the quest for adequate office space, part- or full-time assistance, or better operating budgets, among other needs. NAFA members therefore benefited from the survey in a variety of ways. As you will see, we covered varied topics, including the size of institutions, the multiple duties of scholarship advisors, released time, operating budgets, salaries, "reporting" preferences, institutional support for office space, and Web design.

Since the breakdown of responses appears beneath each question, we are reluctant to interpret the results for others. Like a work of literature, the responses will lead different readers to different conclusions, given the varied needs and missions of their colleges or universities. That was our intention, avowedly pragmatic.

We realize that a project of this sort begs further initiative—to refine current questions or to address those that we may have overlooked. As we hear on graduation day, this is a commencement.

Interpreting the Survey Results

As an example of interpreting the following frequency tables, consider the following:

In the table below, there were five responses to this particular question. Nine respondents did not answer the questions completely. Item number two received one response, which accounts for 20 percent of the total responses to this question. Item number three received four responses, accounting for 80 percent of the total responses to this question.

Example

N=5, missing=9

Response	1	2	3	
Frequency	0	1	4	
Percentage	0	20	80	

THE NAFA SURVEY

What is the nature of your institution?

1. Public
2. Private, non-church affiliated
3. Private, church-affiliated

N=117, missing=4

Response	1	2	3		
Frequency	60	38	19		
Percentage	51	32	16		

What is your undergraduate population?

1. Less than 1,000
2. 1,000–2,499
3. 2,500–4,900
4. 5,000–9,999
5. 10,000 or more

N=117, missing=4

Response	1	2	3	4	5
Frequency	3	22	24	18	50
Percentage	3	19	21	15	43

What is the highest academic credential achieved by your institution's fellowship advisor?

1. Bachelor's
2. Master's
3. ABD
4. PhD
5. Other

N=117, missing=4

Response	1	2	3	4	5
Frequency	11	27	4	70	4
Percentage	9	23	3	60	3

What additional duties, other than fellowship advising, does your institution's fellowship advisor have? Check all that apply.

1. Teaching
2. Honors program
3. Career advising
4. Undergraduate or graduate advising
5. Research
6. None
7. Other

N=255, missing=1

Response	1	2	3	4	5	6	7
Frequency	53	46	21	60	23	10	42
Percentage	21	18	8	24	9	4	16

Are you exempt from most other committee duties because of your various responsibilities as a scholarship/fellowship advisor?

1. Yes
2. No
3. N/A

N=117, missing=4

Response	1	2	3
Frequency	16	77	24
Percentage	14	66	21

If you are a faculty member, do you receive released/assigned time from teaching?

1. No
2. 25 percent or less
3. 50 percent or less
4. 75 percent or less
5. 100 percent
6. N/A

N=111, missing=10

Response	1	2	3	4	5	6
Frequency	16	4	7	4	0	80
Percentage	14	4	6	4	0	72

About how many hours do you devote to scholarship/fellowship responsibilities on campus between normal work hours each day?

1. 1–2
2. 3–4
3. 5–6
4. 7–8

N=111, missing=10

Response	1	2	3	4
Frequency	50	23	16	22
Percentage	45	21	14	20

How many "after-hours" and weekend hours do you devote to scholarship/fellowship work per week?

1. 1–5
2. 5–10
3. 10–15
4. 15–20
5. 20–25
6. 25 or more

N=111, missing=10

Response	1	2	3	4	5	6
Frequency	76	18	13	1	2	1
Percentage	68	16	12	1	2	1

Does your institution have a dedicated fellowships advising office (with or without staff) or is fellowship advising part of the ongoing activities of a larger office (for example, honors program, undergraduate services, etc.)?

1. Separate office
2. Part of a larger office

N=115, missing=6

Response	1	2
Frequency	32	83
Percentage	28	72

What work-study or staff support do your fellowship advising office or advising activities have?

1. None
2. Part-time staff/some work-study
3. Staff shared with others
4. One full-time staff member
5. More than one full-time staff member

N=116, missing=5

Response	1	2	3	4	5
Frequency	38	32	33	7	6
Percentage	33	28	28	6	5

Does you institution provide Web design support and maintenance for your fellowship office of activities?

1. Yes
2. No

N=115, missing=6

Response	1	2
Frequency	71	44
Percentage	62	38

Do you have adequate office space in which to conduct your fellowship advising?

1. Yes
2. No

N=117, missing=6

Response	1	2
Frequency	77	38
Percentage	67	33

What is the operating budget (excluding salaries) for your fellowship office or activities?

1. Less than $2,000
2. $2,000-$4,999
3. $5,000-$7,999
4. $8,000–10,999
5. $11,000 and above

N=113, missing=8

Response	1	2	3	4	5
Frequency	54	18	16	8	17
Percentage	48	16	14	7	15

What is your base salary?

1. Less than $30,000
2. $30,000-$39,000
3. $40,000-$49,000
4. $50,000-$59,000
5. $60,000-$70,000
6. Above $70,000

N=114, missing=7

Response	1	2	3	4	5	6
Frequency	7	23	27	25	11	21
Percentage	6	20	24	22	10	18

If you are a faculty member, would you retain that base salary if you were not the fellowships advisor?

1. Yes
2. No
3. N/A

N=109, missing=12

Response	1	2	3
Frequency	28	3	78
Percentage	26	3	72

Do you receive a supplement to your base salary for working as a fellowships advisor?

1. No
2. 10 percent
3. 20 percent
4. 30 percent
5. 40 percent or more
6. N/A

N=115, missing=6

Response	1	2	3	4	5	6
Frequency	60	4	1	1	0	49
Percentage	52	3	1	1	0	43

If you have a nine-month base salary, how many hours per week during the summer do you devote to administering your office or to advising?

1. None
2. 1–10
3. 10–20
4. 20–30
5. 30–40
6. 40 or more
7. N/A

N=111, missing=10

Response	1	2	3	4	5	6	7
Frequency	2	14	3	2	0	3	87
Percentage	2	13	3	2	0	3	78

Have you taken a cut in pay to be a fellowships advisor?

1. Yes
2. No

N=112, missing=9

Response	1	2
Frequency	9	103
Percentage	8	92

For how many years has your campus sponsored fellowships advising?

1. Fewer than 2 years
2. 2–4 years
3. 4–6 years
4. 6–10 years
5. More than 10 years

N=114, missing=7

Response	1	2	3	4	5
Frequency	20	24	10	15	45
Percentage	19	21	9	13	39

How many years has your fellowships advisor been at his or her current institution?

1. Fewer than 2 years
2. 2–4 years
3. 4–6 years
4. 6–10 years
5. More than 10 years

N=113, missing=8

Response	1	2	3	4	5
Frequency	30	29	7	12	35
Percentage	27	26	6	11	31

To whom do you report?

1. President
2. Provost/Vice President for Academic Affairs
3. Dean/Associate Dean
4. Honors Program Administrators
5. Other

N=115, missing=6

Response	1	2	3	4	5
Frequency	2	29	47	20	17
Percentage	2	25	41	17	15

Does the university official to whom you report understand the importance of national scholarship competitions and of the work that goes into mentoring prospective applicants?

1. Yes
2. No

N=112, missing=9

Response	1	2			
Frequency	96	16			
Percentage	86	14			

To whom would you like to report?

1. President
2. Provost/Vice President for Academic Affairs
3. Dean/Associate Dean
4. Honors Program Administrators
5. Other

N=111, missing=10

Response	1	2	3	4	5
Frequency	2	48	36	15	10
Percentage	2	43	32	14	9

For purposes of his or her annual review, should the scholarship advisor, if a faculty member, be assessed by his or her:

1. Home-base academic department
2. Central administration
3. Both

N=98, missing=23

Response	1	2	3		
Frequency	14	27	57		
Percentage	14	28	58		

Does your institution show support for all competitions, rather than for just the more glamorous ones?

1. Yes
2. No

N=114, missing=7

Response	1	2	
Frequency	89	25	
Percentage	78	22	

Does your institution do enough to facilitate the undergraduate research projects that so often help students advance in national scholarship competitions?

1. Yes
2. No

N=115, missing=6

Response	1	2	
Frequency	74	41	
Percentage	64	36	

Notes

Chapter One: Reconnection, Responsibility, and Renewal: The Rhodes Trust and the Mandela Rhodes Foundation by John Rowett

1. The best assessment of Rhodes is provided by Robert Rotberg, *The Founder: Cecil Rhodes and the Pursuit of Power* (Oxford: Oxford University Press, 2002).

2. Anthony Kenny, ed., *The History of the Rhodes Trust 1902–1999*, (New York: Oxford University Press, 2002). The Rhodes Trustees have commissioned the noted historian Philip Ziegler to write a history of Rhodes and the trust that bears his name.

3. The Right Honorable Don McKinnon, "Multilateralism and Multiculturalism—the Commonwealth in the Twenty-first Century," (lecture, Oxford Centre for Islamic Studies, Oxford, England, 2002).

4. John Battersby, Sunday Argus, February 16, 2003.

Chapter Eight: Elocution Lessons? An Ethical Approach to Advising by Suzanne D. McCray

1. The following was adapted from a talk given at the 2001 NAFA conference in Tulsa, Oklahoma.

Chapter Ten: Strengthening Nationally Competitive Scholarships: Thoughts for an International Conference in Bellagio by Alice Stone Ilchman, Warren F. Ilchman, and Mary Hale Tolar

1. A revised paper may be found as a chapter in Alice Stone Ilchman, Warren F. Ilchman, and Mary Tolar, eds., *The Lucky Few and the Worthy Many: Scholarship Competitions and the World's Future Leaders*, (Bloomington: Indiana University Press, 2004).

2. See Harriet Zuckerman, *Scientific Elite: Nobel Laureates in the United States*, (New Brunswick, N.J.: Transaction Books, 1996, 248–254).

3. Robert K. Merton, "The Matthew Effect in Science," *Science* 159 (1968): 56–63. "For unto every one that hath shall be given and he shall have abundance; but from him that hath not shall be taken away even that which he hath."

4. See, for example, Pierre Bourdieu and Jean-Claude Passeron, *Reproduction in Education, Society and Culture,* (London: Sage, 1977); Pierre Bourdieu and Jean-Claude Passeron, *The Inheritors: French Students and their Relation to Culture,* (Chicago: University of Chicago Press, 1979); Pierre Bourdieu, *Homo Academicus,* (Palo Alto, Calif.: Stanford University Press, 1988).

5. See http://www.fordifp.net/.

6. See "DAAD, Annual Report 2000/2001 Summary," (Bonn, Germany: Deutscher Akademischer Austauschdienst, 2001), 9. The numbers associated with the European Union's Erasmus/Socrates program are, literally, too large to comprehend and because of the fundamental commitment to "European academic mobility" might be considered as a special case. See Ulrich Teichler, "Student Mobility in the Framework of ERASMUS: Findings of an Evaluation Study," *European Journal of Education* 2 (1996): 153–79.

7. See Anthony Kenny, ed., *The History of the Rhodes Trust 1902–1999,* (Oxford: Oxford University Press, 2001), chapter 1. Will is reprinted pp. 568–78. Instructing those panelists who would weigh these criteria in their choice, he initially gave 40 percent to literary and scholarly attainments and 20 percent each to the other three. In a later codicil he modified the allocation, reducing academic qualifications to 30 percent and raising to 30 percent the qualities of courage and concern for the weak. In other words, a young man from the United States, Germany, and the then Empire educated at Oxford and selected competitively on the basis of a record of leadership, concern for justice, strength and resilience, and ability to do the academic work at Oxford would more than likely provide the public leadership Rhodes sought. The Scholars were to be selected without regard to creed or race and limited only by the basis of number for each area, such as two for each state and territory in the United States. See also Jeffrey Stewart, "A Black Aesthete at Oxford," *Massachusetts Review* 93 no. 34 (Autumn): 411–428; Robert Bruce Slater, "Black Rhodes Scholars in Academia," *Journal of Blacks in Higher Education* 2 (Winter 1993–4): 102–7; Frank Aydelotte, *The Oxford Stamp and Other Essays,* (New York: Oxford University Press, 1917); Laurence A. Crosby and Frank Aydelotte, eds., *Oxford of Today, a Manual for Prospective Rhodes Scholars,* (New York: Oxford University Press, 1922); Lord Elton, ed., *The First Fifty Years of the Rhodes Trust and Rhodes Scholarships: 1903–1953,* (Oxford: Blackwell Press, 1956); Thomas J. Schaeper and Kathleen Schaeper, *Cowboys into Gentlemen: Rhodes Scholars, Oxford, and the Creation of an American Elite,* (New York: Berghahn Brooks, 1998); Don K. Price, "A Yank at Oxford: Specializing for Breadth," *American Scholar* 55 (1986): 195–207; and the many research reports, yet unpublished of Profs. Theodore Youn and Karen Arnold of Boston College.

8. See "DAAD" 9–10.

9. Robert J. Sternberg and Elena L. Grigorenko, "WICS: A Model for

Selecting Students for Nationally Competitive Scholarships" (paper presented at Strengthening Nationally Competitive Scholarships conference, Bellagio, Italy, November 6–9, 2002).

10. Alexander Astin, *What Matters in College, Four Critical Years Revisited,* (New York: Jossey-Bass, 1993).

11. Richard J. Light, *Making the Most of College,* (Cambridge, Mass.: Harvard University Press, 2001).

12. For instance, Ernest Pascarella and Patrick Terenzini, *How College Affects Students,* (New York: Jossey-Bass, 1991).

13. Two of the authors have eighty years of higher education experience between them.

14. Astin. The "Intellectual Self Esteem" peer group is defined by self-reported academic achievement, and abilities in leadership, public speaking, writing, aspiration, confidence, etc.

15. Light 44.

16. Light 88.

17. Astin 233.

18. William Bowen and Derek Bok, *The Shape of the River,* (Princeton, N.J.: Princeton University Press, 1998).

19. Astin; Light.

20. Astin 431.

21. Personal communication to Alice Ilchman from Allan Goodman, October 8, 2002.

22. Allen Neuringer, "NSF Graduate Fellowship Evaluations," *American Psychologist* 48 no. 8 (August, 1993): 913–5.

23. http://www.stanford.edu/dept/icenter/orc/scholarships/rmintro.html and http://www.stanford.edu/dept/CDC/students/jobhunt/Rhodes/sld001.htm.

24. An exception is Friedhelm Maiworm and Ulrich Teichler, "Study Abroad and Early Career, Experiences of former ERASMUS Students," *Higher Education Policy Series* 35, ERASMUS Monograph No. 21, (London: Jessica Kinglsey Publishers, 1996).

25. Personal communication.

26. Personal communication.

27. http://users.cyberone.com.au/myers/rhodes-scholars.html; http://www.geocities.com/CapitolHill/Senate/1777/rhodes.htm; and http://www.davidicke.net/tellthetruth/research/rhodesscholars.html.

28. The Princeton Class of '55 Project provides an ambitious example of connecting recent graduates to public and social service through mentored internships.

29. See, for example, John Berry, "An Evaluation Framework for the Commonwealth Scholarship and Fellowship Plan," *Commonwealth Secretariat,* August, 1994.

30. Maiworm and Teichler.

31. Catherine P. Ailes and Susan H. Russell, *Outcome Assessment of the U.S. Fulbright Scholar Program*, (Washington D.C.: SRI International, 2002).

32. http://www.markle.org/about_markle/foundation_history/index.php

33. Hans Rosenhaupt, "Report on Woodrow Wilson Fellows, 1945–77" (given to the Ford Foundation, January 9, 1978); Susan Uchitelle and Robert Kirkwood, "The Danforth and Kent Fellowships: A Quinquennial Review," (presented to the Danforth Foundation, St. Louis, April 12, 1976).

34. See http://www.fordifp.net/.

35. Michele Lamont, "The Evaluation of Scholarship Programs," (paper presented at Strengthening Nationally Competitive Scholarships conference, Bellagio, Italy, November 6–9, 2002).

Chapter Eleven: Keys to the United Kingdom by Elizabeth Vardaman

1. All members of the panel provided notes used in aspects of this report. I am particularly indebted to Mark Bauer for contributing not only important content, but also keen perceptions, and considerable editing skills.

2. Representatives from the following universities attended: Ball State, Baylor, Brandeis, Carnegie Melon, Colgate, College of the Holy Cross, Columbia, Darthmouth, Denison, The George Washington University, Indiana University at Pennsylvania, Kansas State, Muhlenberg College, Ohio University, Penn State, Pomona College, Smith College, United States Air Force Academy, University of Arkansas, University of California at Davis, University of Colorado, University of Illinois at Chicago, University of Massachusetts at Amherst, University of Mississippi, University of Scranton, Villanova, Yeshiva University, and Yale.

3. For example, 85 percent of Rhodes Scholars now take graduate programs at Oxford. Two one-year master's degrees, such as law and environment, combine well for some students on two-year fellowships such as the Marshall. Other students may elect to follow a one-year master's degree with a year of supervised research.

4. See Glossary, Appendix B.

5. In order to present as accurately as possible the materials as they were provided to us during the trip, I have relied heavily on a resource which many of the NAFA travelers have valued greatly. It is a detailed diary of the substance of the meetings held during week one in London, Cambridge, and Oxford. NAFA is deeply indebted to Mary Lee Ledbetter of Holy Cross University, who graciously shared her notes with the group. Her twenty-nine-page record of week one was printed in full in the 2003 NAFA Denver conference notebook. Insights from her missive are quoted throughout this document and noted as Ledbetter in the notes with page references to the full text in the NAFA notebook. The Web references, where needed, have been updated.

6. Ledbetter, 14. The history of and explanation of the assessment process

is found at http://www.qaa.ac.uk/revreps/subjrev/assessingquality.htm and states that six aspects of a program are graded on a four-point assessment scale (1 to 4), in ascending order of merit: "Curriculum Design, Content and Organization; Teaching, Learning and Assessment; Student Progression and Achievement; Student Support and Guidance; Learning Resources; and Quality Management and Enhancement. A 24 is highest score possible on a TQA.

7. Donald McLeod, who helped produce the *Guardian* League tables 2002, reminded us that the league tables are set for taught courses, not research courses. The *Guardian* receives over a million hits a month on the League tables Web site. Ledbetter, 15.

8. Fully appreciative of the detail with which these grids are designed and implemented to evaluate teaching and research, Monro quipped at one point, "Only the British could devise a seven point system that runs from 1 to 5."

9. Ledbetter, 14.

10. For full details on Monro's description of the Prospects Web site, see Appendix B.

11. Ledbetter, 15.

12. Ledbetter, 23.

13. Ledbetter, 26.

14. http://www.pomona.edu/ADWR/Fellowships/home.shtml.

15. Ledbetter, 3. These notes were taken during an overview summary of English higher education given by David Van de Linde, Vice Chancellor of Warwick University. Professor Van de Linde also noted that among those universities that had been granted "old" status were universities created in the 1960s, including Warwick, Bath, Sussex, and Surrey.

16. Ledbetter, 6. There notes were based on a presentation by Mary Denyer of the Association of Commonwealth Universities, who spoke about the Marshall. Many NAFA members agreed with Denyer's point that we need to encourage students to research their subjects and program beyond the "golden triangle" of London, Oxford, and Cambridge. Several NAFA members said this insight was one of the most important understandings they gained during the trip.

17. The culinary skills of Oxford Brookes professionals received a 5* rating from NAFA members, who were given a delicious sample of delights from the gourmet kitchen at a beautiful luncheon.

18. Beatrice Merrick, Director of Services for the UKCOSA provided the overview of UKCOSA—which has kept the UKCOSA acronym despite the change of official name to The Center for International Education. Helpful links to internet sites for British Council, EducationUK, Higher Education and Research Opportunities (HERO) and others can be found at http://www.ukcosa.org.uk/pages/studentlinks.htm. The twenty-eight pamphlets (ranging in topics from practical tips to immigration to finances) are found at http://www.ukcosa.org.uk/pages/guidenote.htm#choose.

19. Ledbetter, 6. The pamphlet "Sources of Funding for International Students" details scholarship options, including the Overseas Research Students Awards Scheme (ORSAS), and can be downloaded at http://www.ukcosa.org.uk/images/studyuk.pdf.

20. Dag Hammarskjöld, *Markings*, (New York: Alfred A. Knopf, 1964), 89.

Index